EDUCATION
for
LIBERATION

Adam Curle

JOHN WILEY & SONS, Inc.
New York

First published 1973
© 1973 by Adam Curle
Published in the U.S.A.
by John Wiley & Sons, Inc.
New York

ISBN 0 470–18950–9

Library of Congress Catalog Card No. 73–13309

Printed in Great Britain

Contents

In affectionate gratitude
to the participants in my seminars
at Harvard University

Introduction

During the past few years I have come to realize with increasing conviction that there are only two tasks worthy of human time and effort: the purification of one's own nature and the service of one's fellow man (which is perhaps the same thing as the scriptural injunction to love God and one's neighbour as one's self). So far as the first is concerned, there is little we can do on our own; it is therefore incumbent on us to turn our capacities to the second. This means, essentially, that we try to create conditions in which the fewest obstacles are placed in the way of people coming to terms with themselves. War is one such barrier. So is great poverty, so are oppression and exploitation, so is hunger, so is chronic disease, so is emotional sickness. If all these things were abolished, every human being would still be faced with his own greatest inner obstacles but he would be more free to make the attempt to surmount them.

I have for many years been deeply, if often mistakenly, involved in attempts to overcome poverty, ignorance and social degradation. For the last six or seven years I have also been engaged in efforts to prevent people, on a massive scale, from killing each other. At length, painfully, I have arrived at a network of ideas concerning development and conflict resolution or – as I prefer to call them, uniting the process – making peace. This, as I have tried to describe it (Curle, 1971, 1972), comprises a sequence of procedures which can be applied to any relationship from that of a man and woman in marriage to that of nations at war. Here I concentrate on a particular relationship (or set of relationships – the more closely one studies anything the more complex it appears), the education or learning relationship. To what extent does it help or impede us in our prime human tasks; how far does it promote peaceful and how far unpeaceful relationships; to what extent does it bind us to attitudes which are narrow, selfish and materialistic, and how far does it liberate us from them? And if it is not of signal help in the fulfilment of our human work, can it be changed for the better – and if so, how?

This explains why I have called this book *Education for Liberation* (but titles are never as comprehensive as one would wish). My concern, however, is more for the human condition in general than with some more specifically pedagogical goal. This is in no sense a teacher's manual which might help him to cope with classroom problems, as are some of the admirable works to which I refer later. I have tried to show that the world's largest industry, which has the greatest opportunity to sow in our minds and those of our children the seeds of peace, justice and equality (the three being, to me, mutually supporting if not synonymous), sows more the seeds of destruction. The tares outnumber the blades of corn. I am not optimistic about reversing the proportions. At least, however, it is easier to do something about education – especially if one is a teacher – to take some small concrete action, than to affect an arms race or an immoral war; and if enough people do it, a difference will be made.

I have written these pages during the summer of 1971. My family and I have been living peacefully in an old farm-house in the woods of Maine, but every morning we have listened to the radio news of wars and rumours of wars. We have been particularly moved – my wife and I met and courted there – by the atrocious events in East Pakistan, Bangladesh as it now is. Twice I have been poised to go there, but feared there was little to be done. I lived for several years in Pakistan as an adviser to the government, firstly on social affairs in general, latterly on education, on which I wrote a book. I was hopeful that the educational plans we devised on would bring greater stability to the country and greater equality and opportunity to the mass of the people. It has not worked out like that. Although there are, of course, ignorant fanatics in the army, the leaders – as I knew them at any rate – were brilliant and cultivated men: once again we learn the bitter lesson that a high level of education may accompany a low level of humanity. In this sorry case education has less to do with peace than with deep and unfeeling prejudice and the callous calculus of self-interest. This short book attempts to show how education might indeed conduce to peace. But it would be a different form of education in a different sort of society.

I have been thinking about this book, in a rather general way, for some time. My concentration began to focus on it, however, while conducting a seminar (called Awareness and Identity) based on my previous one. The problem I posed was: how might these ideas affect educational practice. We tackled the question from many angles and I am deeply in the debt of the many students whose wisdom and experience helped me to see new things, or old ones more clearly. I am also most grateful to the Dean of the Harvard Graduate School of Education, Ted Sizer,* for years of friendship and support in doing things which were really a nuisance to him. What Ted did at work, my wife Anne did at home (and helped with my writing as well): I am a most fortunate man. Julie Turkevich and Pat Jacobson typed this book at the last from tapes I sent from Maine to Harvard. I greatly appreciate their good-humoured intelligence and thoughtfulness.

I should finally note that in writing this book I have been plagued by the problem of pronouns. It is conventional but deplorable to refer to people collectively as 'man'. It is, however, cumbersome to refer continually to 'men and women' and to 'he and she' or 'her and him', etc. We really need some pronouns that refer equally to both sexes. In their absence, however, I have tried to avoid sexism in my writing, for example by referring to teachers in the plural rather than to a single teacher who must be either male or female. When this has been unavoidable, however, I have tried to alternate the sex of the teacher rather than to make the text clumsy with the continual use of 'he or she', etc.

* He was succeeded in 1972 by Paul Ylvisaker, another man of warmth and humanity.

I

The Context of Education: The System

Education enslaves: men and women become free through their own efforts. This harsh fact, which challenges half my life's work, has been inexorably brought home to me – the conclusion drawn inescapably from so many failures and miseries and from the occasional shafts of light throughout the world.

Only ten years ago I wrote a book about developing countries which ironically sold rather well, propounding the opposite thesis. The wide spread of education, I argued then, would open men's minds; they would become aware of their capacities; they would become aware of what they were being denied by poverty or class or race; and they would surge forward to become themselves and to take their due. Education would thus become a great levelling force, levelling, so to speak, upwards. I realize now that education, *as it is mostly practised*, does not so much free men from ignorance, tradition, and servility, as fetter them to the values and aspirations of a middle class which many of them are unlikely to join. In my earlier book I also connected education with economic development, the assumption being that education also inculcates the attitudes and skills which increase productivity; thus the more education, the more wealth. There is some truth in this hypothesis, but the arguments are complex, ambiguous and moreover now irrelevant to me because I have reached an understanding of development of which the keystone is justice rather than wealth.

My disillusionment with education was gradual. The first stage was the recognition that, in the Third World, it was far from mobilizing the spirit of the masses. On the contrary it tended to establish a new *élite* alienated from and frequently prepared to exploit those masses: those who had the luck or influence to go to the better schools and on to the universities became rich but the condition of the majority, if anything, became worse – there are more hungry people in the world today, even proportionately, than twenty years ago. This linked up with the second stage of my awakening: the realization that, despite all apparent efforts, economic development was not – except in a few places where perhaps oil had been found – being achieved. Admittedly education had not been considered as a key factor in development by everyone or even a majority in the field, but to the extent that it might be credited with some effect the expansions of the 1950s and 1960s seem to have had no impact.

But I am not only concerned with the Third World; this book is about education in general. There is, perhaps, a more measurable relationship between education and economic growth in such countries as the U.S.A., but if what is happening in the few very wealthy nations is development – and it is by most conventional criteria – is it really what we want? The biosphere is being destroyed by pollution, the earth's resources are being used up at a catastrophic speed, violence is rife, racial disharmonies intensify, the poor countries are despoiled to feed consumers' appetites made ravenous by advertisement appealing to the middle-class ethos, the poor at home are neglected, youth is alienated, material prosperity is inextricably intertwined with increasing production of perilous armaments, endless and purposeless wars are waged.

Education has a three-fold part in creating this form of 'development'. Firstly, and obviously, it supplies the necessary technology. Secondly, it inculcates an attitude of mind which accepts the system which produces these awful symptoms. Of course most people dislike most of the symptoms, but they fail to perceive the relationships which produce them; if they did so they would also have to reject the prizes which they receive from the system and upon which the comforting affluence of their life is based. Thirdly, education has the opposite effect of holding back segments of the population, of preventing them from entering into competition with their betters, of keeping them poor and useful to the *élite* even when the *élite* is the majority. This may seem strange, but the slum schools of Britain, America and other wealthy nations are not so much gateways of opportunity as training grounds for failure: 85 per cent of black and Puerto Rican children in New York schools are functionally illiterate after eight years of education.

Such considerations changed my views on both education and development. I came to see that the meaning of development depended upon one's vantage point. If one profits from loans or investments, whether national or international, one perceives the fact as developmet, but if one's condition remains the same or deteriorates, figures for economic growth are mere meaningless statistics. Development to most people is still basically an economic concept. The experts will demur, maintaining that development involves the general development of society. But no one is quite sure what this means and they still behave as though all that mattered, with perhaps a few caveats, were economic change. I am now brought to the point where I believe it is imperative to start from the other end (and am encouraged that a few people whom I respect, like Julius Nyerere, have done the same) and to proclaim that the object of development is to create a form of society in which all human beings may live with peace, dignity, and satisfaction. In order to achieve this sort of society there has, obviously, to be an effective economy, but there are some things which could be done to strengthen the economy which would weaken the harmony of society and would not, therefore, ideally be permitted.

Instead of being hopeful about education, I began to see it in its total effect to be hostile to what I see as development. Here I must add a softening word. Much education and many educators, far from being evil, are very good: they impart the eternal (and the contemporary) verities with compassion and wisdom. But the thrust of formal schooling, of the educational hierarchy, of the curriculum is, I believe, anti-developmental. To succeed educationally is, essentially, to acquire the skills and congruent attitudes for *economic* development, that is to say

3

acquiescent participation in the technological advance and the social callousness which has marked the material progress of the West. These attitudes might be summed up under the term competitive materialism. The successful products of many educational systems then take their places in what might be termed the exploitative network. This comprises the political, economic, and industrial organizations of the powerful whose power enables them to take advantage of the powerless. The rich, whether nations or individuals, are potential exploiters since they have the power to strike bargains which are to their own advantage and the disadvantage of others, thus flouting justice and diminishing their dignity. Only those with a strong sense of morality can resist the temptation to make use of power for their own ends, and I would find it hard to argue that nations have a collective morality based on altruism. The exploitative network is a network because the *élites*, which mostly means the educated *élites*, of the poor nations are sucked into the rich countries' economic systems. They serve as the local agents for the great corporations or as the officials who facilitate their cancerous growth. In so doing they gain much personal profit, whatever happens to their country. Their education has certainly helped them and they would seek the same scholastic advantages for their sons, but the gap between the rich and the poor countries widens. On a global scale the rich nations are streaking away in terms of wealth from the poor ones (and suffering pollution and other ills in consequence): within the poor nations the gap between those engaged in the modern sector of the economy and those engaged in traditional pursuits, chiefly agriculture, is widening comparably and for the same reason.

This book is intended to show how education might, but usually does not, contribute to peaceful relationships. Up till now I have been expressing my disappointment with the role of education in development or social change, but my work in this field also drew me a few years ago into situations of conflict, in two cases bitter armed conflict on an international scale. I saw how futile and fragile were our hopes when all we have striven for could be swept away in a brief uprush of violence. I also

4

perceived, which was even more disturbing, that many conflicts arose out of efforts purporting to be developmental but which, whether or not they achieved their professed objectives, created imbalances, inequalities, and tensions, stirred up old resentments and created new ones. Education was frequently a factor, although indirectly, in these situations.

For some time a great deal of my energy was devoted to exploring ways of resolving such conflicts. In a way this was non-intellectual work because when people are dying one acts first and analyses later, but part of my mind was always grappling with the underlying questions: why do these outbreaks occur; what can we do to forestall them; what have we done to create them? Eventually, and helped by more critical thinkers, I began to see that large-scale violence was but the culminating point of a sequence of situations in which there had been provocation, jealousy, oppression, exploitation, neglect, and the like. The violence could be hard – killing, wounding, threatening, or soft – economic exploitation, emotional manipulation, cultural deprivation, failure to take available steps to succour or to protect, emotional or material enslavement. These are small circumstances in which one party to a relationship, the weaker, is impeded through the quality of a relationship from achieving his human potential. If soft changes to hard violence, as it easily does, he may be killed, which effectively curtails his development. In other circumstances, involving perhaps a 'Victorian' family with an arbitrary and authoritarian father, or a minority group, the damage may be complex and various, ranging from psychological to physical. Oppressed groups, such as the black people of South Africa, commonly live less long, are more often sick, lose more infant children than do their overlords. I call such relationships unpeaceful for the dual reason that they are inherently anti-human and they often lead to massive outbreaks of overt violence. There are, of course, other sources of conflict and violence. If two men fight over the same inheritance or two nations over the same territory there is not necessarily a backlog of oppression and exploitation of one by the other. As we look around the world, however, we can see unpeaceful relationships

5

of an exploitative and oppressive character on every side, on large scale and small. And even where the situation seems, as did in its initial stages the Arab–Israeli confrontation, a relatively straight (albeit most complex) conflict of interests, the machinations of the exploitative network soon muddy the issues.

Education is vitally concerned with all these unpeaceful situations because oppression, exploitation, and other top-dog techniques of keeping on top require two things from education. First is the knowhow to do the job, whether it is drawing up a concession agreement for extracting minerals, or making cheap products to sell expensively to those who have no choice, or building sophisticated armaments. Second is the complex of values I call competitive materialism which is the psychological backbone of the exploitative network in which the knowhow is put to use.

As I became increasingly involved in questions of peace, violence, and the resolution of conflict, I became increasingly aware of another factor which I came to see as having supreme importance in human affairs. This was awareness, meaning primarily awareness of the self but secondarily awareness of, sensitivity to and compassion for others: no one can feel with delicacy about others if he is confused or anxiety-ridden or paranoid or grandiose or abject about himself. All these and other modes of not seeing oneself straight get in the way, like a screen of dirty glass, of one's perception of one's fellows. I learned much about this in the context of interpersonal relationships while working at the Tavistock Institute of Human Relations in London in the late 1940s and the early 1950s. Earlier, however, I had learned about a different approach to awareness. I had read widely in Oriental mysticism, travelled for some time in the Middle East and met interesting dervishes, and I had studied under Ouspensky. The awareness which these types of experiences emphasized was of a much more interior and personal type which I have referred to elsewhere (Curle 1972) as supraliminal awareness.

Much more recently, in dealing with persons suffering from acute strain of violent and dangerous situations, I have found that their sense of their selves was likely to be impaired. Anger at the enemy, fear for themselves and their families, guilt, horror at responsibility for slaughter all made it increasingly hard for them to view themselves calmly. In consequence they constructed an image compounded of the trappings of rank, position, influential friends, honorific offices, and titles, and so on, and all this constituted a sort of citadel to which they could retreat when threatened by self doubt. If I am all these things, they seemed to be saying to themselves, surely I must be wise, brave, mature, magnanimous, etc. But I found that if one is talking to an image of this sort, very little real business gets transacted.

I subsequently followed up these ideas about awareness, terming the image belonging-identity, which seemed an accurate description since the image was fashioned of what 'belonged' to people (titles, properties, handsome husbands or elegant wives, cultivated tastes in wine), or what they belonged to (a regiment, a culture, a club, a profession, a learned society). The stronger belonging-identity, the weaker, obviously, the awareness. There are some people in whom the former seems completely dominant. One can never reach the real person or the inner self, or even an honest fragment of the self. In others, awareness rules, and here there is a combination of wisdom, effectiveness, and humanity. But from my observations it would seem that the median mode of humanity is low awareness coupled with strong belonging-identity. (I should hasten to add that although I began to identify these categories in people under stress, they were by no means median people.)

The relationship between belonging-identity and competitive materialism is obvious. The more splendid the ingredients of our self-image, the more securely we will be protected from the ravages of *angst*, guilt, and impotence. Thus what we *have* is transmuted into what we *are* (or what we try to feel we are). Therefore, we *need* more in order to *be* (or to feel) more and will strive ferociously to outdo each other in the achievements, attainments, and possessions which will establish us most firmly in general opinion, but primarily in our own, as persons of worth. Thus, despite the chicanery, exploitations and cut-throat double

7

dealings we may be impelled to employ, it is possible, paradoxically, that we shall feel relieved of shame and guilt.

I have tried to sketch the interlocking factors – the exploitative network, competitive materialism and certain approaches to economic development, unpeaceful relationships in which the powerful diminish the potential of the weak, low awareness and the belonging-identity which, supported by education or certain facets of education, constitute a lethal system responsible for much human suffering. It is, alas, a system which is extremely widespread. It is exemplified most precisely by Western capitalism, but it is shared in great measure by most communist regimes which, whether they acknowledge it or not, pursue the same goals driven by the same demon. When I refer subsequently to 'the system' I mean precisely this interlocking of social, psychological, and economic factors, and not a vague, emotive abstraction such as 'the Establishment'.

I must make it quite clear that when later I come to advocate a form of education which not only fails to support the system but aims to destroy it, I am also advocating an alien form of society. It would be a society little interested in the vast ego-edifices of the belonging-identity, in extravagant consumption, in competition, in display, in status, rank or professionalism. It would value equality, justice, compassion, the idiosyncrasy of every human being, the possibility of personal evolution. The reader may treat this, according to his taste as subversion or sentimentality. So far as the first is concerned he is right. We have seen the monstrous ills to which the system has brought us; my generation, unlike any earlier ones, has seen the combination of rapacity, blindness and pride propel mankind to the edge of the abyss. (I stress, however, that I do not despair about mankind; men have created wonderful things – but they are not part of the system and I pray that they survive the system.) As for sentimentality, if it means to strive for something better, then I am sentimental. I hope I am also realistic. I have grappled too long with our world's intransigent problems to believe in easy solutions, or to have much hope that the system will collapse.

THE COUNTER-SYSTEM

But the system is not completely dominant. Embedded in our society and, one might perhaps say, our nature is an entirely opposite sequence, a counter-system. In the system, as we have seen, a low level of awareness is associated with the development of a strong belonging-identity; from this derives a motive which I term competitive materialism; this dominates a wide range of our human relationships, making them – by definition – un-peaceful, that is to say, we use those involved in the relationship for our own ends rather than their own, manipulating them emotionally or exploiting them politically or economically; finally, these relationships become crystallized and perpetuated in the form of institutions such as capitalism, class and political structures based on power, and the exploitative network. (This sequence is presented linearly, but it is more properly circular, for the institutions and forms of relationship undoubtedly affect the level of awareness and the type of identity.)

The counter-system is an equally connected sequence, but awareness, to begin for purposes of comparison at the psycho-logical point of the continuum – is higher. Being more in touch with ourselves, we are less dominated with the half-sensed guilts, anxieties, angers, feelings of inadequacies and unworthiness, and therefore less driven to compensate for them by an identity in which by acquiring things – possessions, people, money, exotic tastes, imputed qualities – we are able to feel that we are not so bad. But with higher awareness our self-image is based more upon what that awareness reveals of our nature (awareness-identity), than on what we amass in order to conceal further that nature from ourselves. The accompanying motive has not the self-protective character of competitive materialism with its obverse of using others. It will tend to be based more on altruism. This is because when we are less preoccupied by our own emotional needs we have greater empathy with others. When we are not deafened by the clamour of our feelings, we can hear the inner voice of others; we are able to enter into their sufferings and hopes, to *feel* them. It is possible that this potential for sensitivity to others is not always transmuted into altruism, but it is certainly true that without it both the desire and the capacity to serve them are infinitely less. The human relationships entered into by persons of higher awareness are in general peaceful, because there is not the driving need to use others to assuage the inner hurt; by the same token – at least at this psychological level – there is no conflict of interest and we can therefore be more readily loving and unselfishly supportive. These relationships become formalized in institutions which are co-operative and egalitarian – indeed democracy in its ideal and virtually unknown form could be said to represent the counter-system.

The relationship between system and counter-system can be set out as follows:

FIGURE: *System and Counter-system*

	level of awareness	mode of identity	motive	dominant form of relationship	institutions
SYSTEM	lower	belonging-identity	competitive materialism	unpeaceful (conflicted) relationships, manipulative at inter-personal level, socially and politically exploitative	competition, imperialism, capitalism, class and political structures based on power, the exploitative network
COUNTER-SYSTEM	higher	awareness-identity	altruistic and empathetic	peaceful (unconflicted), loving and supportive	co-operative and egalitarian, democracy in its best forms

The system is of course stronger than the counter-system – the world would not otherwise be in its present pitiable state. Moreover, higher awareness is a fragile growth. It rises and falls, and in those who seem to possess it to an unusual degree it is perhaps only a fraction of what it might be. But the fluctuation of levels of awareness gives cause for hope, because although it may fall in those whom we would consider to have high awareness, it may rise in those whom we consider to have low awareness. It is still more important to recognize that system and counter-system are not phenomena at work somewhere out there; they are within each one of us and are interwoven in every relationship and institution in which we are involved. At one level the inter-action, one might even suggest the struggle, of the system and counter-system is very intimate, very personal; at another it involves the remotely impersonal clashes of ideologies and institutions.

This is not to say, I hasten to add, that all clashes of this sort are between system and counter-system – on the contrary. The struggle for dominance between its components constitute one hallmark of the system. Although at times, as in the relations of the U.S. and U.S.S.R., this struggle may be masked by ideology.

Most education, but not all of it, supports the system. How-ever, many individual teachers, administrators and others con-cerned with education throughout the world are against the system. If they have not yet precisely identified what it is they oppose, closer understanding of the issues would encourage them to act differently as teachers. This will of course be difficult if not impossible in some cases. Where the system is tightly knit, the teacher who propounds the contrary value and ideas of the counter-system will be considered a revolutionary and must accept this hard role or else give in. In other places, however, the atmosphere may be more favourable, and much may be done. Can this undermine the system? That, of course, is too much to expect, but it may have some effect. I have no patience with those who maintain that the society cannot be changed unless the economic system is changed and the economic system cannot be changed unless the labour unions are changed and the labour unions cannot be changed until the law is changed, and so on. Changes are brought about by people who try to influence the segment of life they are involved with, strengthening the rela-tionships and institutions that promote the counter-system –

hopefully if the educators do their part, then economists, politicians, lawyers and the rest will be comparatively active. We may have to operate with and within the existing facilities and take what opportunities are offered to make changes, however small, in the right direction.

The curse which the system has brought upon education is that instead of nourishing man's heart and mind and then releasing them to soar creatively, it binds them to its service. Education enslaves and the world's free spirits have either had an unusual schooling or have learned to be free and open despite their experiences in the classroom. In the pages which follow we will firstly consider the process of enslavement and then the qualities for an education for liberation. Specifically, it would need to counter competitive materialism and low awareness. More positively, it would require the qualities necessary to build a new society which, as we have tried to define these terms, was both developed and peaceful.

2

Varieties of Scholastic Enslavement

There are so many books saying how bad education is, that this chapter should be easy to write. But it is not. To blame bad education for our own ills would be to choose a popular whipping boy, already lashed to ribbons by Holt (1966), Silberman (1970), Kozol (1967) and numerous others. I maintain, however, that it is our best institutions, the finest and most advanced schools and universities, which serve the system most efficiently and bind us most tightly with silken threads. The poor institutions also serve the system in a minor way by producing for it less-accomplished but also necessary servitors. When we hear talk of reforming or upgrading institutions it simply means raising the level, but not changing the type of the product. We shall eventually discuss ways of educating persons who will have no interest in serving the system in any capacity, but who will be eager to work for the establishment of another form of society, one which is in my terms peaceful.

In the meantime I shall try to show how most educational institutions, good and bad, traditional and contemporary, serve the purposes of the system. I have decided to do this by giving examples, fictitious only in so far as they are composites, of different types of schools.

WINTON

This is a highly exclusive private secondary school for boys in England, America, or, with various minor modifications, several European countries. It has a superb scholastic record and a very high standard is required of applicants. It used – it is an old school – to be very snobbish, and thirty years ago most students were sons of alumni or others with equally high status. But now, according to the policy of recognition of the aristocracy of talent, a phrase taken from a speech by the headmaster, there are no social bars to acceptance and there is a liberal scholarship policy for helping promising children from poor families. (This almost matches the fund for helping scions of 'good' families, who have fallen on evil days.) In fact, the number of scholarship children is small. For one thing, the primary schools that serve most poor areas simply do not have the scholastic quality to prepare their students for the gruelling entrance requirements of Winton. For another, working-class parents rarely feel comfortable about sending their sons there.

The teachers at Winton are exceptional. Unlike most of their professional colleagues, they are excellently paid, and the school has thus been able to attract men (and a few women) who have high academic qualifications and would have been able to get university jobs, but really preferred teaching boys. Let me dwell on the teaching. It is in general what might be called progressive. The classes are small and there is a great deal of individual instruction. Every effort is made to discover the students' intellectual growing edge. Once they have acquired interests, they are given every encouragement and much freedom in developing them. The teachers are more like older colleagues than instructors. It is not surprising that by the time they are ready to go on to the university, many have made significant progress in academic work, including such unusual – for a school – fields as microbiology, Chinese poetry or Nilotic anthropology.

Nor is Winton purely cerebral. On the contrary, the whole man is cultivated, and the gifted scholar is likely to be also a competent footballer and a keen violinist, or an adept at hatha yoga and a sculptor. Nor is it an isolated ivory tower; eminent figures from public life, scholarship, and the arts, are frequently invited to talk before the societies which have proliferated to match the varied student interests. The students themselves, who are some of the most mentally alert young people in the world, frequently and fiercely debate the burning issues of the day. In addition, they undertake vacation work among poor communities or join voluntary organizations working overseas.

All this takes place within an ethos of co-operation, permissiveness and equality. There is no caste system among the boys, no exclusiveness among the teachers.

From memories of my own schooling in what purported to be one of the best English schools, I think of these youngsters with envious wonder. True, our teaching was good enough, after we had ploughed our way up through several years of pointless and repetitive assimilation (I was 'taught' *Twelfth Night* seven times, but no other Shakespearean play: that's how the academic schedule worked out). True also that there were good facilities for sports, art and music, but the atmosphere was arrogantly superior. The teachers were well-meaning, capable, but for the most part narrow, didactic and aloof. The boys lived a separate life, like some unpleasing primitive tribe, bound by convention of age sets, cruel initiation, meaningless taboos whose infringement was punished by ritual flogging, secret languages, all these ingredients being welded together by smug and unimaginative snobbery. There could be no doubt that my school served the system. It produced regiments of successfully blundering generals, many haughty proconsuls to shore up the Empire overseas, judges, politicians and civil servants to do the same at home, and a host of business and professional men who voted the right way, held the right opinions, had the right friends and thus helped to maintain the system based upon privilege, possessions, and exploitation.

How, one may ask, can I possibly compare my school with Winton, so magnificently different and superior? To answer this, it is necessary to say something more about the system. It is not something rare and awful facing us today for the first time. On the contrary, it has existed in most places for a large part of history, although, if we are to believe Weber, Tawnay and others, it has intensified since the Reformation and the rise of the middle class. What makes it particularly dangerous today is that it has developed terrific technological muscles which it has

15

not learned to control. (This is not to say that there are no societies without the system even today. Tibet was such a one until recently and there were other theocratic examples in the past. Tanzania is trying to be one, as is China, and there are still a number of tribal and village societies almost untainted by the system, which is otherwise virtually global.) The system is old, widespread, and intricate. It penetrates every cranny of our lives, so that even when criticizing it we are forced to use its own terminology. In view of its size, context, and power, it demands an extremely wide range of servants from the most brilliant versatile stars, to the dumbly obedient routine performers. Winton produces the stars – the great administrators whose weekend delight is playing in a quartet with members of the local orchestra, the Nobel prize winners who effectively enter politics, the successful executives who write children's stories on the side. My school produced the next level, the highly competent professionals who lacked, however, the additional dimension of an imaginative or artistic insight.

It is easy enough to see why I and my fellows served the system. For one thing, there was no alternative model: other views of life were hardly known, or if known were ridiculed. There were only half a dozen possible careers and they all depended upon the system. The tradition of the school, the headmaster's Sunday sermons, our ritualistic reverence for the war dead, all turned us in the direction of honourable membership of our class (middle to upper middle) and hence service to the system.

In an unexpected way the students of Winton are equally constrained. The atmosphere, of course, is far from conservative and every possible topic is debated freely. Many of the boys profess to hold radical views and my old headmaster would have reached apoplectically for his birch rod (yes, this was employed even in my era) if he had heard any average discussion of sex or drugs.

But for all its libertarian and progressive policies, Winton turns towards and depends upon the system, just as the system needs these brilliant young people whose soon-to-be-forgotten foibles are part of the process of growing up. The syllabus, diverse and flexible though it is, is geared to the universities and the universities are directed towards consolidating the knowledge and inculcating the skills which are necessary to the system. Moreover, the young princelings of Winton can hardly help but be influenced by what awaits them. They know perfectly well that their membership of this select establishment will, of itself, open many doors and that if in addition they are academically competent and generally accomplished nothing can stop them. But the educational excellence of Winton strengthens the idea of hierarchy and privilege, whether based on birth, as in the past, or ability, as is now the policy. At this point, however, I have to say that to their honour, as well as to the horror and the confusion of their elders, an increasing number rejects these prizes and searches for a different manner of living; this, however, they have learned in spite of Winton.

I am here suggesting something which is central to the theme of this book. Almost every type of education including the best, the most humane, liberal and intelligent, serves the system, because it imparts knowledge needed by the system and because it establishes goals within us (goals which can be achieved through the right use of knowledge within the system) which are also of value to the system. But before pursuing the implications of this suggestion, I want to portray some more schools.

XVILLE HIGH

This is an average secondary school which might be almost anywhere. It is average in every respect; the quality of the teachers, the family background of the students, the academic standards. Those of the students who proceed to college go to institutions of average quality and achieve average results. They go on to 101 jobs which are necessary to society, and of course many of them come back to school as teachers – almost, one might think, as though they have never left. But the work they do is, for the most part, not of a very high order. They might be termed the second echelon people. They serve as the assistants, the number two men to the Winton graduates. As among the latter, at Xville High there is a high correlation between the levels of family, school, and subsequent employment. There are naturally exceptions, but the total ambiance of Xville High makes for mediocrity.

To start with fundamentals, the school is controlled by a committee of the city council (most schools throughout the world in what are termed democratic nations are ultimately under the authority of elected representatives of local or national bodies). Most people, whatever their politics otherwise, are educationally conservative. They value good behaviour – which means conformity – rather than inquiring minds. They are frightened lest the liberty and new ideologies of education turn the children from the ways of the parents or make them lose interest in 'good' jobs and 'sound' careers. They distrust educational policies which would change the existing social pattern (as by bringing in more children from minority groups) and the elected representatives of the community must heed these views if they wish to be re-elected. Thus school administrators and senior teachers, if not from conviction, then for survival and perhaps eventually from habit, give in to pressures to abandon originality in their teaching, to give extreme emphasis to the outward manifestations of discipline – there must be no talking, no running, no visits to the toilet without signing in or out – to suppress questions, to permit no intellectual initiative on the part of students, to adhere rigidly to a set of ancient and no longer – if they ever were – meaningful rules.

There is great stress on hierarchy; in fact much of the discipline is designed to emphasize the inferiority of children to adults – they are a different sort of animal, foolish, malicious, and irresponsible. They can only be motivated by a competitive system of awards and punishments, taking no account (which is perhaps understandable in the circumstances) of any possible interest they might have in their studies. In one sense, this system works. It does, in some students at least, promote a scrabble for good grades, not only to please the all-powerful and arbitrary teacher, but also to get a little more leverage within the school hierarchy. For although the teachers remain implacably separate, a little of their status rubs off on the 'good' student. I had not realized how inextricably interwoven in 'western' education are competition and hierarchy until American Indians told me of their experiences in government-run boarding schools. The hierarchy was racial and obvious, for the teachers were white. The competition was so natural to them that it took someone from another culture to remark it. There were, of course, grades and other types of distinctions, but what struck the Indians more forcibly was that when the teacher wished to motivate them, she would say, 'Let's see who can sit up straightest, make his desk tidiest, finish first,' all of which was anathema to a culture in which it is the height of discourtesy to push oneself forward or to show up another's difficulty or defects.

The instruction imparted in these conditions tends to be abstracted from reality and life. Literature is not studied to be enjoyed, but as a subject for the most mechanical tests: who said what to whom when; what is the derivation of this word; when did the writer die? History and other social studies are narrowly biased topics written from the point of view of a particular nation, culture, and epoch. It might be thought that more concrete topics, such as the natural sciences, would fare better, but this is not the case, because they depend upon an atmosphere of free inquiry which Xville High successfully eradicates – even if any survive from the previous ordeal of elementary education.

This is not to say, however, that school fails to teach anything. On the contrary, the children learn to be docile, passive, and conformist because that is the way to get through without trouble. They learn to be thoroughly distrustful of adults because they work to a pattern which is arbitrary, cruel, and irrational. Children clearly see this adult illogicality. I recall that when fourteen I won the school poetry prize. But at the same time I was being held back because I was 'bad at English', having failed to grasp a method of torturing sentences into their component parts. This seemed to be a ludicrous contradiction, but it was part of the distastefully inexplicable yet omnipotent and unchangeable adult world. I simply gave up trying; what, I asked myself, was the use. Children learn that the point of education, if any, is to play the teacher's game, to find out how he likes one to sit or ask questions, what are his particular idiosyncrasies, what amuses him, what irritates him. All this is not to say that everyone dislikes school. Although many hate and fear it, others enjoy playing the game and like the privileges that can come with doing so skilfully. And the ultimate prize is a diploma, which will give easy access to higher education, or a job. The high-flown idea, so common at Winton, that education should widen and enlighten the mind, would be regarded by most Xville students – rightly in view of their experience – as farcical.

There is nothing in this education – except for the few who may be shocked awake by its absurdity – to promote awareness. Its values of conformity, of playing safe, of disparaging what, from another point of view, is creative and free, strengthen a belonging-identity of a somewhat crude type. The most readily available image is of someone who has done well in the prevailing middle to lower middle class culture. Among older students this will mean having an attractive boy or girl friend, access to a smart car, smoking a popular brand of cigarette, sporting a particular style in hair and dress (other cultures will have other symbols – the principle is the same). The structure but not the strength of the identity is easily transmuted in later years when the components become well-behaved and achieving children, a wife who belongs to the right committees or a professionally successful husband, membership in a lodge or an exclusive club, and so on and so on with again modulations for other cultures. The force of competitiveness has already been referred to and its material focus is ensured by the nature of the teaching.

Xville High, in short, supports the system well. It supplies – or it would be more accurate to say strengthens, since there is a continuum of impetus from family to school to family – the motive force to preserve and serve a materialistic, competitive, and essentially conservative society. The alumni and alumnae of Xville High are great patriots. They cannot afford the liberal internationalism of Winton alumni (which nevertheless does not prevent them from urbane exploitation of poorer nations) but they have been conditioned to believe fiercely and mindlessly in the values of what they do possess. Not having, for the most part, really very much, they feel threatened by those who do not share their values. Different values jeopardize what they have, thus endangering their belonging-identity. Hence arises a hostility (which in turn affects the school committee and thus the administrators and teachers) to long hair, hippies, communists, blacks, or whoever it might be.

SCHOOLS OF FAILURE

Our examples so far have been of schools which, in their several ways imparted competitive materialism, supported the exploitative network, and impeded the growth of awareness, thus positively strengthening the system and weakening the counter system. The Winton products, with their intricate versatility and great knowledge, play the major parts; they are the Renaissance men. The former students of Xville High play lesser parts, even very small ones. The knowledge they have to sell is less valuable, and their personalities are less well attuned to the subtleties of this world. But they support and need each other and to some extent share the rewards of the system.

A competitive system, however, requires constant losers against whom the others can measure their success; and the materialistic system needs the advantage of exploitation; and the system based upon the psychological element I call belonging-identity needs a group which confirms its goodness and reality. For these reasons the poor, particularly those who are differentiated by reason of race, language, religion, etc., are very necessary to the system, not as even the most junior partners, but as people to be used by it.

For this reason, there has come into existence a type of education which I call the school of failure, which not only prevents its students from joining the system, but even tends to reconcile them to their condition. Annie Stein (1971 pp. 158–9) remarks that 'the average child in 85 per cent of black and Puerto Rican schools is functionally illiterate after eight years of schooling in the richest city in the world', (New York) and goes on to add, ironically, that 'this is a massive achievement' on the part of the educational authorities. It is the result, according to her analysis, of stratagems devised 'by an oppressive racist and exploitative society' in order to preserve these unhappy qualities and the institutions upon which they depend. Her diagnosis of our society and its motives is not unlike my own, except that I believe my analysis is more pessimistic: she is interested in improving education and is rightly angered that so little has been done; I am interested in a more radical transformation because I believe that improvement of the sort that she refers to will only strengthen the system.

The strategies referred to by Mr Stein are firstly control through Containment. This form of control was exercised for many years through segregation and continues to this day in the *élite* academic high schools, which are almost exclusively white. As the movement for community control began to develop, however, a new kind of strategy emerged. This was to discredit new proposals for community involvement as 'black racism' and 'reverse apartheid', and led to the teacher strike of the school year 1968-9. Today's central control over segregated schools remains as strong as ever; the strategy has worked well.

The second strategy was to Train Teachers to Fail. This means to drum into them the idea that the children in their schools are really incapable of learning, have no ambition, no verbal stimulation, no visual stimulation, are culturally deprived, belong to the culture of poverty, have no curiosity, possess weak self-concepts, and so on. Such views, vigorously propounded by social scientists and imparted to teachers, have the character of self-fulfilling prophesies. If we expect children to suffer from these disabilities and treat them accordingly, it is not surprising that we have difficulty in teaching them to read, or indeed to do anything else.

Mr Stein calls the third strategy Institutionalized Mechanisms for Failure – A Magic Bag of Tricks. The tricks include tracking, a discriminate system of categorizing children according to very dubious academic criteria; a curriculum watered down to meaninglessness for supposedly below-average children; a tendency for teachers to urge children to drop out, 'Why not get a job? You'll never learn anything here'; almost complete lack of accountability; and so on.

All this contributes effectively to preventing the poor from breaking out of the vicious circle of poverty, of entering the system and competing with its more powerful members.

Paulo Freire (1970), writing of the different context of Brazil (and the Third World in general) talks of literacy programmes based on blandly meaningless and irrelevant phrases such as 'Mary likes animals', or 'Charles' father's name is Antonio. Charles is a good, well-behaved and studious boy', or 'Eva saw the grape', which confuse and obfuscate social reality and dull the consciousness of the learner with alienating words. The Brazilian illiterates are, like the New York blacks and Puerto Ricans, marginal to society, to the system.

My friend Peter Scharf tells of the humiliation inflicted by comparable educational programmes for young adult offenders in which the reading material is suited for seven-year-olds and old-fashioned ones at that – all stories of dolls, fairies, and children playing with kittens. This is education employed, consciously or not, to prevent those of whom society has in effect wiped its hands from re-entering the system. They remain its permanent whipping boys, its awful example of the coincidence of crime, illiteracy and cultural deprivation, its zero from which the success of competitive materialism can be measured.

ACHIPONG

I conclude these descriptions with a different type of story. Achipong is an *élite* West African school with a long tradition and a high repute. It was established by genuinely altruistic Europeans who wished to bring the Africans the best education that Oxford or the Sorbonne (you may take your choice) had to offer. The colonial government gave it every support because the school produced young people who became by temperament and

23

outlook closely identified with their rulers and very happy to serve them, albeit in subordinate capacities. These results were achieved by removing the girls and boys from their tribal villages and placing them in boarding houses, by inculcating the appropriate ethos of competitive sports and scholasticism, by teaching them an entirely European curriculum which, apart from the language, stressed, exclusively, the history, geography and literature of England (or France). And this was accepted because in the humiliating colonial situation the only way to power in any degree is through sharing, though subordinately, in the colonial power – and in so doing one is alienated from one's heritage.

The alumni of Achipong were prominent in the independence movement, but the intellectual weapons they used had been forged in the cultural centres of Britain and France and a strangely symbiotic relationship compounded of resentment and affectionate subservience grew up between them and the colonial rulers. When they achieved independence, the Achipong *élite* took over the colonial system completely and assumed not only the roles but also the ethos of the colonialists. They felt as benignly superior to their unlettered fellow countrymen as the French (or English) had towards them, and the gap between them was as great.

The colonialists and their fellows from the rich countries had not of course really gone. Though no longer nominally in charge, they maintained an economic stranglehold. The country in which Achipong is situated was not important to them as a place to settle (the climate was too bad), but they wanted to retain their influence. There were useful minerals they could purchase cheaply because they had the financial whiphand and there were markets for their own much more costly products for the same reason. In addition, they hoped to keep the communist influence out, and wanted to preserve a strategic base. For these purposes, the metropolitan nation kept its claws in the country. Loans and grants were given which whetted, but never satisfied, the appetite for industrial and agricultural development, for roads, telecommunications and schools. In return, conditions were exacted which bound the former colony more firmly to the economic coat-tails of the former ruler. The main export was to be sold at penal rates, an excessive quota of imports was to be accepted, 'understandings' were reached about voting at the United Nations, and so on. The government could never break away because if they had done so, they would have sacrificed their ability to satisfy the constituents who, because the rulers doled out clinics or kindergartens or veterinary services with the help of foreign aid, voted them in.

This is not to say that the Achipongs were all disillusioned and resentful. On the contrary, many of them were doing extremely well as local employees of great European or American companies, or as the favoured officials who facilitated their operations.

What might be termed the Achipong ethos has permeated the rest of the country. In the lesser schools which have proliferated, the same goals are sought; a European education and a share in the limited affluence derived from the neo-colonial affiliation. Many failed to make the grade because available jobs have not expanded as rapidly as hoped, but they seldom returned to the village life of craftsmanship, agriculture or animal husbandry from which they had been estranged by their alien aspirations.

In general, the rural areas remain depleted and impoverished, *vis-à-vis* the towns where live the lettered *élites*, just as do the poor countries as a whole *vis-à-vis* the rich countries – and for the same reason: the exploitation of those who have not by those who have.

The former students of Achipong, and their humble brethren too, have been imbued with competitive materialism and drawn into the exploitative network. The result, so far as their country is concerned, is not development as I have tried to define it (see pages 108–9). On the contrary, the lot of the majority is worse than it was. Like the American blacks and Puerto Ricans, they are outside the system and although we may be thankful for the lack of corruption, we must pity the material suffering.

I have outlined several types of education in the attempt to show that they all, including what most of us would consider the best, combine to enslave us and to create unpeacefulness which I also term the perpetuation of a system based on the belonging-identity, unawareness and the operations of the exploitative network. Even in the schools for failure, whose products hardly enter the system, the main complaint is that they do not acquire the capacity to do so.

But not everyone is enslaved. Some, who knows from what core of inner strength, reject the blandishments of the system despite its most attractively presented allure and maintain the tough but tenuous structure of the counter-system. Others have received a different element in their education. We shall subsequently examine what this might have been.

COMMENTS ON SCHOOLS

The driving force for most education is service to the system. This is not to say that very many teachers do not teach what they believe to be of value to the personal growth of the student or to have intrinsic importance of its own. Nor is it to deny that very many students are fascinated by the process of learning, for its own sake. But the total context within which this learning and teaching takes place is one in which young people are being prepared for roles in a competitive society, that is to say, they are acquiring attitudes of mind, knowledge and qualifications (these last two not always being identical) which enable them to operate within the system. The system, being competitive, materialistic and unpeaceful, is by the same token hierarchical. There are, as we have seen, hierarchies of schools (and, of course, of universities) fairly closely but not absolutely, corresponding to hierarchies of class and occupation. If you attend Harvard, Oxford, or the Sorbonne, or their principal feeder schools, you are more likely to end up as a high business executive, a lawyer in an important firm, an academic in a powerful university or a highly paid engineer than as a garbage collector, a truck driver or a shop assistant – these jobs are reserved for the products of schools for failure or for the less successful alumni of Xville

High. The latter, we also feel, however much we may intellectually deny it, to be less good, less worthy human beings. The more successful alumni of Xville High may also become professional men, academics and the like, but they will tend to earn less, to work with less plushly upholstered companies, or less renowned universities. Thus an education which serves the system serves also to perpetuate its inequities. There is, of course, some movement up and down, socially, educationally and in terms of employment; but this is of value to the system rather than the reverse, because it emphasizes competition and a striving, however futile in most cases, to better oneself. In fact when knowledge becomes a commodity, as Ivan Illich (1971) (1971a) frequently and eloquently urges us to understand, society becomes professionalized, unequal and unjust; we enter the mad race of technical proliferation because productivity, novelty and hence conspicuous consumption have become the criteria of generally accepted worth. And education – or rather the badges which education confers – helps us to excel in that race.

I would emphasize here that the subjects we learn or are taught are not in themselves bad. There is nothing wrong about the study of philosophy, economics, history, natural science, mathematics, psychology, engineering, medicine, etc., etc. What is bad is that our knowledge, or supposed knowledge of these subjects, is a piece of capital with which we buy a partnership at one level or another of the system. If our capital is small, the level at which we enter the system insures, in all probability, that we will be almost permanently subordinate to those who have more capital in terms of high degrees at *élite* institutions. (And they have more capital, usually, because their families have more actual money.) But however small their investment, they will be at a level above the students of the schools for failure, who are not properly in system at all.

The ethos of the system and its educational institutions is interlaced with certain ideas about human nature and human abilities. Of supreme importance for many years and in some respects still today, was the concept of intelligence, that elusive quality which, when measured, purported to predict how well a

27

child was capable of doing in school under favourable conditions. But it eventually began to be held, as one cynic put it, that a high I.Q. predicted only the ability to do well in intelligence tests. Nor was good work in school or even college necessarily a promise of comparable future achievement. On the contrary, as Liam Hudson (1964) has entertainingly demonstrated, the undergraduate records of neither Darwin nor Einstein would today have qualified them for a grant to do graduate work. Of greater significance in predicting subsequent development than high I.Q. are such qualities, David McClelland suggests, as perseverance, energy, creativity, leadership, interest and emotional stability.[1]

However, even if we accept this wider concept of the prerequisites for eventual success, we are still operating within a context of achievement as the criterion for that success. This means, essentially, success in the system. It cannot mean otherwise so long as we fail to discriminate between education as the personal enrichment of the individual and education as the commodity which enables him to buy into the system. Other ages and some societies existing today have been able much better than we to differentiate between, on the one side, the trappings of power and success and, on the other, such qualities as wisdom, sanctity, purity, moral strength, or inner unity and to value the latter quite separately from the former. I would not suggest that as individuals we have no sensitivity to these qualities, but as a civilization – and the system represents a sort of global civilization – we pay only lip service to them. What counts is success. Consequently, we value not only the skills required for success, but equally the attitudes of mind which harness these to our advancement. Thus the vicious circle revolves, linking the education to the attitude to the materialism to the competition to the low awareness to the education. All this adds up to the existence of an unpeaceful society in which the advantage of some is achieved at the expense of the disadvantage of others, and to

[1] In discussion with myself. I am not sure whether the distinguished author of *The Achieving Society* (1961) has ever directly expressed these ideas in writing.

the development of an education which blinds and enslaves us.

If we are to change this situation, to break out of the vicious circle, we must above all begin to think differently about human beings. Of what are they really capable? Which of their potentialities should we most value? How may these be better realized through education? Such queries and their answers certainly involve values, but so do all discussions of education. A good education is what best promotes what we believe to be right; thus the best education in Nazi Germany was that which most effectively produced good little Nazis. I have based the earlier arguments in this book and its two predecessors in this series on a concept of peace which is value-based. The concept of human nature which I shall now outline is closely related to it.

Human beings are capable of living peacefully together. It is not a psychological necessity for them to be continually scrabbling to get on top of each other, to prove themselves stronger or clever and to feel virtue in so doing. They can have much higher awareness and hence a greater sensitivity both to others and to social injustices. Ardrey (1966), Lorenz (1965) and others may point to powerful pressures working in the opposite direction, and they are no doubt, in some senses, correct. It would be absurd to argue, however, that people cannot be more peaceful (to use a compendium word for these qualities) than most of us are. We can each of us find, in our own experience, examples of individuals who are exceptionally peaceful. These are the people who neither exploit nor manipulate others, but who relate directly and altruistically to them without interposing demands and conditions arising out of their own inner needs; they are, in my terms, people whose awareness-identity is strong. Such individuals are found in every culture, but there are also, it seems to me, whole cultures which tend to be more peaceful than the predominant Western civilization which, through the exploitative network, has become so all encompassing. What I would call peaceful cultures are co-operative rather than competitive and display a considerable collective concern for the welfare of individual members of the group. Such cultures are not, or were not, uncommon (see Mead (1961) for an interesting analysis), but unhappily for the world they are small and lacking in influence. I have personally encountered remarkably peaceful cultures among the Lapps of Northern Europe, some West African village communities, the Chakmas of the Chittagong Hill Tracts (see Curle (1971), pp. 97–102), and certain North American Indian societies. I am not, of course, arguing that all 'unspoilt' or rural societies are peaceful; often the contrary is true and I have known some, such as the Pathans, who straddle the borders of Pakistan and Afghanistan, who have a life style in which violence is a major component. My point is simply that unpeacefulness is not an inescapable quality of individual and group life. By the same token, it should be possible to expand and strengthen peaceful behaviour. I believe that education as we mostly practise it weakens peace, but that education as it might be practised could strengthen it.

3
A Possible Future

In this chapter, and those which follow it, I shall work backwards. I begin by trying to describe what I believe would be the ideal educational system for a truly peaceful society, one which was as congruent with peace as what we have at present is with unpeace and then consider how it might be attained. The ideal, of course, is utopian; we shall not achieve anything comparable within many lifetimes. The exercise is not irrelevant, however, because if we are clear as to the ultimate goals, we can more easily perceive the intermediate steps, which I shall discuss later, by which these goals may be more speedily approached.

A PEACEFUL WORLD COMMUNITY

Let us try to assume that this community, albeit perhaps fragile, has been achieved. It is peaceful in my sense in that there are no (or fewer or greatly reduced) social relationships of oppression or exploitation or of course of actual violence and that by the same token competitive materialism has been greatly diminished (I would not attempt to suggest the monstrous upheavals by which such a change has been wrought; that is for the futurologists. For the purposes of my argument, we will simply assume that it may happen in some far tomorrow so that we may better act today to make it more possible. This means that people are less rapacious, for the belonging-identity is equally weakened and they do not have to prove their worth or to compensate for their inner doubts by frantic acquisition. In consequence, the earth's resources are less ruthlessly pillaged, pollution is greatly reduced and technological developments are limited to what will substantially improve man's lot. But what will be meant by improvement differs from what it does today. Our age views it as an amelioration of our condition if we can get faster from one place to another, or see a brighter colour picture on our T.V set, or be persuaded that we really need something that we had previously been quite happy without. Improvement in the future will mean the increasing perfection of man's nature. Whatever we may mean by this, whether we mean some form of spiritual evolution, or the realization of our variety of potential talents, or our deepening inner harmony, or any combination of these, technology has little contribution to make. Perhaps the best that it could do would be to remove what might be adverse physical conditions, to prevent famine and other natural disasters, to eradicate debilitating diseases, and to make more readily available the riches of the mind and human creativity – the music, the stored knowledge of libraries, the artistic masterpieces. But the keynote of such a society would be sufficiency of housing, food, warmth, health – for the development of the human person. Excesses such as we now strive for are not only unnecessary, but anti-developmental. They tie up too much energy, they deplete the environment, they concentrate too many hopes and emotions, they absorb too much of us whether we achieve them or we only try to. But in this future society, men and women would need less. They would, therefore, be more free to create, to become more fully themselves, to develop increasingly deep and mature relationships with each other. This would, in fact, be the world of the counter-system.

THE SCHOOLS

The purpose of the schools would be, so far as possible, to set the children on the road to being whole and peaceful human beings. Their basic task would be to help their students to come to terms with their own nature. That is to say, to develop greater awareness of themselves, and thence by stages of the world and society within which their nature was realized. It would not in

32

the least be to buy the knowledge necessary to enter the system as we know it.

While I would not wish to limit or prescribe the studies relevant to the basic purpose (the syllabus might contain many of today's subjects, but their presentation would be geared to individual idiosyncrasy), I would emphasize that they would be learned in a completely different context. There would be no grades, diplomas, degrees, failures or successes, or other preliminaries to entering – or not entering – the system in some professional or technical capacity. By the same token there would be complete lack of competition: how could we be competitive about actualizing ourselves? There is no set standard for self-realization because our patterns of potential development are as richly diverse as life itself. It could be argued that the lack of competition makes for slipshod work and it is true that the desire for success or fear of failure may spur people to some sort of great effort. But we know perfectly well that the most valuable work comes from interest (and good teaching which arouses interest) and we also know that nothing destroys interest more effectively than to push children inappropriately. I must emphasize that lack of competition does not imply the lack of excellence. Indeed I believe that the form of education we are about to consider is more likely to achieve excellence – though perhaps of diverse sorts – than what our children presently endure.

In trying to describe this form of education in imaginative outline, I have to admit that I know little about how to impart it. In any case, if ever a truly peaceful society comes into existence, so many things will be different and will have been different for so long that our contemporary basis of understanding may be quite inadequate for predicting its character and operations. Nevertheless, one has to start somewhere. My own sketchy beliefs about how to promote this sort of education are outlined in the next few chapters as the steps which can be taken now, in the context of all our present disabilities, to implement the future. The rest of this chapter is concerned with what might be the final results of what we could start doing tomorrow.

33

THE TEACHERS

Certainly everything will depend upon the quality of the teachers. It always has done, of course, but now that education is so vast an industry and the standards of teaching so various, many students learn more from good books than from poor teachers. For the sort of education which I envisage, however, supremely good teachers are indispensable. They must be able to sense the latent capacities, the potential lines of development, the inner blockages and confusions, of every child. They must appreciate many kinds of growth, including those which the system today ignores or despises, and recognize that they may represent perfection for a given individual. Finally, they must know what to teach and how, to do so in order to fulfil the potentialities of their students' growth.

A first step towards obtaining teachers who can act in this way would be to disestablish the teaching profession (indeed all professions, as we shall see, but teaching first of all). There would be no profession of teachers, no group of young men and women who have made the choice for good reasons or bad to be pedagogues rather than technicians or doctors or advertising agents, or who indeed had no choice about it at all. The teachers of tomorrow would be chosen in mature years (how old this might be varies from person to person) by a commission skilled in identifying wisdom, patience, sincerity, warmth, and inner coherence. It matters little how such a person has spent most of his or her life – as a stone mason, computer expert, physician, cook, waitress, farmer or poet.

Once selected as a teacher, which would be the highest honour the community could confer, the man or woman would spend some time preparing for the task, repairing deficiencies in actual knowledge of topics they might need to teach about, studying children, learning to manipulate the new media which will have been developed. But these things, which we normally consider the core of teacher training, would merely be the frills. The core for them is the people they are.

One of the differences in the role of the future teachers will relate to authority. We tend today to be very confused about the authority of the teacher. There is one view, which we could consider the conservative (or backward), which holds that the teacher should be considered as the repository of all wisdom, the students being empty vessels into which his erudition is to be poured. It is not for them to question his intellectual or indeed his moral authority. In fact it is not for them to question him at all, except for clarification of some point which, in their ignorant immaturity, they may not have understood. The extreme opposite view, the modern (or progressive) is that the teacher, being an adult, is usually wrong. The intuition or natural good sense of the child, until driven underground by insensitive adult incomprehension, is more reliable than the judgement of the teacher who is already warped by his own experiences. The best he can do is to provide a protective setting in which children can explore new social and intellectual experience without being emotionally oppressed by grown-ups. At this extreme, the teacher has virtually no authority. In the schools of the future, teachers would enjoy the real authority of their personal stature, but people of this calibre also recognize the authority of every human being's autonomy and idiosyncratic identity. Thus in a sense authority is shared, not because of the rigidity of a system or the limitations of an ideology, but because of psychological reality. In fact it would be an important objective of education for students to learn about relations of responsibility and authority by participating in them.

THE CHILDREN

The average child brought up in a peaceful society may differ considerably from those of our own desperate age. While it is undoubtedly true that the process we term socialization is an inevitable and universal element in the development of human beings, societies make different demands for adjustment. The exigencies of the system weigh heavily upon our generation from early years. Our parents are under pressure, our teachers are under pressure, and these pressures are all too soon transferred to us. We learn about how to please those upon whom we depend and to value the rewards of good behaviour, rewards sanctioned by the system and sowing within us the seeds of its values. The rewards, values, and punishments of the system are particularly prone to limit our human scope. If to be good is to conform to the tenets of competitive materialism and hence to place great value on possession and position, on aggression, on conflict, and on hierarchy, we tend to become closed to the inner life and to each other's feelings. Eventually we lose touch with ourselves.

Many young children delight us with their spontaneity, their perceptiveness and their penetrating profundity which pierces the shams with which we try to protect ourselves. It is as though they are open to influences and sensations to which we are no longer receptive, but to which their sensitivity is blunted all too early, by four or seven years of age perhaps. The very young possess a degree of awareness which really places them in a different category from their parents. When Jesus said, 'Unless you become as little children you shall not enter the Kingdom of Heaven', he was expressing not a sentimental liking for babies, but a tough psychological fact. Young children are open, receptive, aware; as the system, through our agency, presses on them, they lose those qualities. They become increasingly overlaid by the patina of socialization. They learn to respond automatically, to react spontaneously to the stimuli of the system, to conform, to compete, to forget themselves in their pursuit of what is outside themselves.

The psycho-physical shakeup of adolescence somehow releases awareness again, reopens a chink in the armour with which society covers us. We are, of course, distressed to find our young people so difficult and unreasonable, but we hope that they will soon 'come to their senses'. What we mean is that we trust they will be recaptured by the aspirations of the system and take seriously their preparation for entry into it. Nowadays, thanks to some mysterious dispensation, the adolescent reopening lasts much longer and seems in some cases to be virtually permanent, though the young themselves believe that most are recaptured by the age of thirty. By that time the attractions are too strong and the alternatives too weak for continued resistance. (This is discussed at length in my *Mystics and Militants*.)

In a society which has, however, been peacefully non-competitive for generations, the socialization process may well be quite different and the influences upon children to close them, to reduce their awareness, much weaker. The promise for education is immeasurable.

TRAINING AND EMPLOYMENT[2]

Because this is a peaceful and non-competitive society, there will be no jobs having either high or low status. It will not be 'better' socially or financially to be a brain surgeon than a plumber, or a road mender than a lawyer. Men and women will do the work they like and are good at or which in some way helps them to come to terms with themselves. Since there will be no compulsion to build up a professional reputation (in order to command higher fees, more prestigious appointments and hence greater possessions and a strengthened identity of belonging), people may change their work in tune with changes in themselves.

Clearly, however, there are many jobs which require training and perhaps all could be done better with some preparation. As well as the schools, therefore, there would be training institutes at which students would be instructed in any topic, from pottery to surgery, from farming to accounting, from physics to truck driving, from librarianship to woodwork, from sculpture to house decoration, etc.

I envisage that the life pattern of individuals would vary greatly. School and training at an institute might be concurrent, or sequential or alternating. Students might, for example, leave

[2] The ideas in this sub-section owe a great deal to Ivan Illich, especially Illich (1971). I am most grateful to him for having pointed out the implications of knowledge as a commodity, but differ from him – I believe – in thinking that schools which use knowledge for self-development rather than employment can serve a very valuable function.

school early, train, practise their craft, return later to school; or they might leave late, having already learned a skill, or they might spend part of their day at work, part at school. Everything would depend upon their inner growth and their education should have made them sufficiently sensitive to it to take willingly the proper action.

This training would be realistic in a sense in which much of our present education and/or training is not. We have gone qualification mad and tend to equate the diploma with the capacity to do the job. The more 'developed' the system, the longer the process of training drags on into early middle age. Yet ironically, at the same time, we have learned how to impart most technical skills in a few months and laugh at the socio-economic system which demanded a seven-year apprenticeship for a craft which could be learned in a few months. We forget nine-tenths of what we learned at school without ever having put it to use and most of what we acquire in college, while much of what we do remember, particularly if technological in character, is obsolete before we have a chance to apply it. The way in which we really learn, in fact, is by reading with interest and discrimination, by discussion with our colleagues, by pondering over intriguing problems, by making mistakes. The myth is that all our useless encumbrance of knowledge activates and matures the mind, enabling it to deal effectively with any type of problem. This was what was said of the classical education in which the great British universities excelled. It may well be true today of Winton, where the interaction of gifted and privileged adults with gifted and privileged adolescents makes for a ferment of intellectual interest. It is, however, emphatically not true of Xville High, where the dreary waste of irrelevant and boring subject matter spewed out to obtain the diploma is voided also from the mind.

We are speaking of a time, however, when knowledge will have ceased to be a commodity promoting entry into the system. The vested interests which currently regulate professional and technical training and so demand payment in dues in the currency of years of study, degrees and the like, will no longer exist. Consequently the training authorities can without fear be perfectly practical in arranging whatever preparation is necessary for particular tasks. Many devices will be used, such as on-the-job training, to break the tedium and frequent obsolescence of institutional training.

CONCLUSION

To sum up, the essence of this education approach is the separation of education – the development of the individual through the cultivation of awareness and of intellectual and artistic potentiality – from preparation for employment. In our society this is scarcely possible. Education is the conveyor belt which feeds workers into the maw of the system; however interested a young person may be in history of Spanish literature, the good degree he or she obtains as a result is a receipt for having paid into the system. Doing well at school is the first step – despite the fact that it may not imply real competence – to being well-placed in the system. But in a truly equal society, in which rewards of money or prestige were no different for one job than for another, achievement in school or university would not be sought eagerly as leading to professional employment and hence high social and economic status. School would have a purely personal value. It would constitute the setting for a highly individual exploration by children of themselves and their world. This would, it is true, lead them to prefer one sort of training to another, but because of its capacity to fulfil and interest rather than to confer position.

Such education is less unusual than may be thought. Many tribal societies have something comparable. The children are removed to what in parts of Africa are called bush schools, for various periods of time, during which they learn how to be mature members of society. They learn the tradition and values of the tribe, the religious rituals and beliefs about the spiritual world; they learn about sex and the responsibilities of marriage and parenthood; they learn how to conduct the affairs of the tribe. But they learn how to *work*, that is, how to cultivate the land, how to tend cattle, to build houses, to work in wood or metal, from their fathers or their uncles. It is worth noting that many of these societies until touched by western influence, were remarkably uncompetitive.

4

The Teacher's Awareness[3]

Now we return from the fantasied world of a no doubt very
distant future to today's inexorable realities. The schools are the
training ground for the system, indeed they represent the system
and are controlled by the individuals and organizations who
control it. Thus one might feel that the educational system is
well insulated from the possibility of alteration, but in this icy
wall of the establishment there are nevertheless footholds for
change.

The individual teachers can perhaps do most to alter from
within the close-geared relationship of school and system. It is,
of course, true that many will, and in fact do, find it very hard to
strike an independent role which might have any impact on this
relationship. Their superiors bear down harshly on them for
unorthodox behaviour and in extreme cases they are dismissed.
Moreover, their problems are often compounded by having no
clear idea of what they are trying to do. They are angered by
discrimination or cruelty or bigotry or the narrowness of the
curriculum, but have not analysed the connection of these
symptoms with the cause, which is the interrelationship of the
variables which I term the system. Hence they do not have a
coherent plan of action and react violently to specific ideas in a
way which makes it easier for the authorities to take action
against them. Thus in a notoriously racially segregated area they
defiantly teach the poetry of a black poet (to quote a famous
case of the 1960s), but they do not see racism as just one aspect

---

[3] The ideas in this chapter are also developed, in somewhat different contexts, in Curle (1971, pp. 209–216), and Chapter 2 Curle (1972).

of a class-ridden and unequal society and realize that the best way of promoting an appreciation of social justice may be through building a just and equal society in the classroom. The flamboyant gesture which makes a martyr of the teacher may have little educational value.

On the other hand, many teachers are in much more favourable circumstances. Their heads and principals are permissive or even sympathetic, the local committee or board of governors may include people of enlightened or sceptical opinions, and the parents may welcome innovating teaching. But here I must be explicit. I am not simply talking about better education, for this may imply no more than a pedagogical improvement which raises the level of entry into the system. This is often as unpopular with the authorities as teaching which directly attacks the system, a fact which illustrates the value of hierarchy to the system. For example, if Xville High teachers were to conduct their classes in the same way as their more exalted colleagues at Winton, they would probably be fired. This would not be because they were flouting the system, but because they were introducing into one level the method and outlook appropriate to another. The parents, controlling committees and indeed most of the teachers of Xville High do not like and feel uneasy with the Winton young gentlemen – when they are mature they respect them as their superiors, but by an odd compensatory quirk of emotional logic are able themselves to feel superior to the wild, militant, and unconventional younger generation. What I am talking about is education which somehow breaks into the vicious circle of competitive materialism, low awareness, strong identity of belonging, and education as a commodity with which to buy into the exploitative network.

A second source of change is the private school. There are through the world many private institutions established by groups who reject the system, or at least certain aspects of it, and are supported by parents holding equally radical views. However, there are very few people who, even if they detest the system, are prepared to give their children an education which provides them with no qualifications – such as entry to the university – to work within it. Thus the private schools, even the most revolutionary, prepare the students to take certificates or diplomas and to that extent are compromised.

The last paragraphs raise two fundamental and related questions. Is there any point in working within the system; and can we work outside it? If the answer to both were no, we might well give up trying and float along with the advancing current of competitive materialism until we were engulfed in one of the eddies to which it is prone. Let us take the second question first. Even the hippies in communes who possess nothing are within the system because they rely upon welfare supplies and unemployment payments. I am certainly in the system because, quite apart from my job as a professor at Harvard, that Winton of Universities, I have money in a savings bank which invests, no doubt, in the great corporations which the system has invented to control its destiny. Most of the revolutionaries are definitely in the system, not only because of affiliations and privileges they enjoy, but because what they want is a change in the power structure of the system through which the poor (or the particular groups with which they are identified) become rich and the rich become poor. I see little merit in such changes; the low awareness, the competitive materialism, the belonging-identity and the exploitation remain just as strong as they were. Like it or not, then, we are in the system. We can, of course, guard against participating in its most flagrant abuses, try to correct the wrongs which come to our attention, act constantly to counter injustice and oppression. But our most important task, without which the others are flawed, is to alter our inner attitude, to increase awareness, to eradicate competitive materialism in ourselves.

Since we cannot readily get completely out of the system (except perhaps by giving up all our possessions and joining some remote tribe), we have to operate within it. Indeed common sense would tell us that the best way to influence education is to be involved with it; from outside there is little we can do except to make speeches and write books or, if we are addicted to violence, to bomb schools – two equally futile activities. True, there are the obstacles I have already mentioned. True also that

43

the differences in the teaching style to which I shall be referring to are not going to turn the school systems upside down. However, a change in the school system (as part of the total system) is not the first objective of the awakened teacher. He or she is engaged in the subtle chemistry of human interaction, and the objective is to raise, however temporarily, the awareness of the students and to exhibit to them something of the human situation they had not previously grasped, to liberate them from emotional and intellectual slavery to the system. What may follow from these efforts is imponderable, unpredictable, and can hardly ever be attributed directly to the teacher, but such are the cumulative, quiet influences which make history. It is the students who have been touched in this way – who in countless fields, in the courts, the businesses, the professions and the legislature, may change and eventually demolish the system, replacing it with something better.

Just how the teacher may exert this influence is the subject of the next few sections. I must emphasize that I am not concerned with how to teach better, in the sense of imparting knowledge more speedily, efficiently or pleasantly. This may be the outcome, but it is not the purpose. Nor am I interested in what is taught, except in the sense that some material, such as history texts which glorify a particular nation, extol its wars, or whitewash its oppressions, is obviously contrary to the spirit of peacefulness. But having excluded such material (and included some other which I shall specifically mention), I am less concerned with what is taught than how. I should perhaps phrase this differently; I am less concerned with what is nominally taught than what is imparted by the manner of teaching, the relationship of teacher to student, and the atmosphere of the school in general. These things do much more to shape the attitudes of children than the social studies, English, mathematics, or science they learn. At present they tend (except at Winton) to engender passivity and conformity, docility and distrust. I shall try to suggest ways in which they might encourage higher awareness and a diminution of competitive materialism. Finally, I am not concerned with what might be called classroom techniques. I mean

44

by this such things as methods of questioning, the use of different media, the division of a lesson (if formal periods are in vogue) between explanation, discussion, questions and written work, and so on. It is not that I consider such things to be unimportant. On the contrary, they constitute the technology of teaching which all teachers should have mastered. One may, however, have mastered the technology, be accepted as a 'good' teacher and yet through the quality of one's relationship with the children teach them – as well as English or Latin – the values of competitive materialism and other things which support the system.

What follows, then, should not be thought of as a teacher's manual but as a discussion of human relationships in the school setting. Our impact on others depends less on what we do than who we are and in that the determining element is our level of awareness. (See Morris (1972) Chapters 6 and 7.) Since this also may be a quality which education of liberation should protect and promote I shall describe it at some length.

Awareness essentially means self-awareness, a person's consciousness of her or his own being. However, what we perceive about the inner world determines what we perceive about the outer. If our self-perceptions are dulled or distorted it is unlikely that we will perceive others clearly and accurately. Likewise, if we can sympathize with our friends it is improbable that we will experience extremes of guilt and irrational self-loathing. Awareness has also a social or political corollary. To the extent that we are self-aware we are liberated from obsessive self-concerns and able to turn towards people and situations outside our immediate orbit. No longer needing to manipulate or exploit them we can view them objectively and altruistically. It is significant that most sensitive and articulate revolutionaries, from Che Guevara (1967) to Germaine Greer (1970), have spoken of this double aspect of awareness – on the one side of self, on the other of the political or group structure, the strength of each depending upon that of the other.

It is perhaps easiest to describe awareness by starting with states of low awareness. These are conditions, experienced frequently by virtually everyone, and by some for the greater part of their lives, in which they have little understanding of their own motives, actions, or the sources of their feelings. In a state of low awareness, we speak and act relatively automatically, without in the fullest sense knowing what we are doing. Changing moods flicker across the screen of consciousness – worry, self-satisfaction, irritation – following some erratic and hidden sequence of emotional discharges. We do or say things which we subsequently regret and observe shamefacedly, 'I don't know what came over me,' or 'I didn't think.' We talk without listening to ourselves, turning on, as it were, the record appropriate to the occasion and letting it speak for us. Above all, we are not self-consciously aware of our own identity. When we are operating at a low level of awareness it is as though we had switched on the automatic pilot and gone to sleep. But the automatic pilot may lead us in a direction we would not have taken had we been awake.

To be unaware also means to live on the surface, to ignore what lies below the top level of consciousness, to neglect the instinctive or intuitive aspect of the personality, to lead a flat, two-dimensional psychic life. But of course to deny awareness of the inner life does not make it go away. It means, paradoxically, that we are the more likely to be dominated by it. The monstrous fears, the guilt, the shameful longings, the celestial visions, the viper, the baboon, and the angel which comprise our inner pantheon make us, through their interrelationships, what we are. To be unaware is to deny our essence. Essence denied turns sour. If we do not act out what we are we cease to be it. The darker and the more frightening sides of our potential become more dominant, because we are not fully aware of them. If we recognized them for what they are they would, contradictorily, change their nature. But since we sense some obscurely, not as elements to be assessed, appreciated, and incorporated into awareness, but as fantasms, grotesque and horrifying, we turn aside, fearing to look more closely. But they are there, the rulers of our being, dictating every mood, every emotional need, every irrational fear and compulsive action. Thus to be unaware also means to be unfree, to lack autonomy, because we have no conscious control over factors which are driving us. Conversely if we did possess this awareness, not only would we be better able to order our actions, physical and psychic, but the determining factors would themselves be different. The essence would no longer be sour. Thus the purpose of most psychotherapy is precisely to restore this type of autonomy. However, it would be all too simple to consider awareness in extreme terms. The obsessional neurotic, the drunkard, the man in what is significantly termed 'a blind rage', are all obvious examples of people who are both, and for the same reason, out of touch with and out of control of themselves. But I am not concerned with pathological exaggerations. They may be useful caricatures to drive points home, but I am referring to teachers who are essentially 'average', 'normal', or 'healthy' human beings. There is no need to show that highly disturbed people lead impoverished lives or bring grief and confusion to their associates. This we already know. What we fail to recognize so clearly is the effect upon our lives and society of the very common, very usual modes of mental functioning such as low levels of awareness. Most of us are relatively unaware much of the time. We do not actually accept it, for this would imply an incompatible degree of awareness of ourselves. We quite simply consider our mental processes, if indeed we consider them at all, to be perfectly all right, to be natural.

Levels of awareness change. We fluctuate for a variety of reasons from higher to lower awareness. Moments of reflective self-consciousness are chased away by nebulous anxieties, threats to self-esteem, or the desire to show off, only to steal back again when the more negative emotion has purged itself. However, although levels of awareness move constantly up and down, people have a centre of gravity, an average level which is higher or lower. It is with the eventual raising of this level through educational experience that we shall be concerned.

People with a relatively higher level of awareness have a balanced view of themselves. They do not, as is frequent at lower levels, alternate between self-glorification and self-abuse. Instead they see themselves more as others see them, people with certain capacities and positive qualities, certain failings and follies. But they do not torment themselves about their inadequacies, nor puff themselves up about their abilities. They try sensibly, but without desperation, to improve their skills and to overcome their defects. Claiming responsibility for neither virtues nor vices, they can afford to be relaxed in carrying out what is their responsibility – the strengthening of the former and the weakening of the latter. When we are at this level of awareness, we are likely to behave as reasonably and as positively towards others as we do towards ourselves. At lower levels, we are more apt to exploit others in order to assuage the anxious self-doubt created by our unacknowledged selves. Because we are only half aware and so feel anxious or inadequate, we seek for confirmation of our potency or realness, or punishment for our sins, by dominating or being dominated. In countless ways we manipulate others to attain relief from the pains of unawareness. The teacher, unfortunately, is placed in an ideal position to manipulate the children whom the school system has placed in his power, to pander to his emotional needs. Virtually without fear of redress he can expose them to his pent-up anxious anger, his irrational quirks, or his need for power through domination; his sense of inadequacy may be assuaged by imposing upon them and making them respond to his whims; he projects the tendencies which he dimly senses in himself, but never explicitly recognizes – laziness, ineffectuality, deceitfulness, and viciousness – on to the children in his care. Thus he exploits them. That is to say, he makes use of them for his own emotional purposes. Children can also pose a serious threat to the anxious unaware teacher. He senses that they are mocking or deriding him, getting at him, undermining his position and authority and indeed it is true that his relationship with them may hold up the mirror: he may be faced with an intolerable – and hence immediately rejected – image of himself as feeble, crochety, or incompetent. This may drive him to extreme lengths of psychological self-preservation at the expense of the children. Such behaviour is, of course, a travesty of the role of the teacher, who should use his relationship with the children to serve the purpose of their growth, rather than his own reassurance.

Persons with a low awareness are not in touch with their inner selves. They feel threatened by the half-sensed aspects of their own natures, the contradictions, the shameful desires, the guilts, the unreasonable fears, all dim and menacing like creatures in a mist. They are things which can neither be acknowledged nor escaped. The most we can do is to strengthen ourselves against them. One technique, so common as to be almost universal, is to build up what I have termed belonging-identity. This is a form of psychological protection which, as I have already suggested, we construct for ourselves out of the things which belong to us, or to which we ourselves belong – our civilization, the traditions of our class or community, our church, academic achievements, handsome husband or wife, successful children (so like their father!), taste in music, important friends, investments, collection of contemporary art, devoted dog, etc. By some process of psychic fabrication we build from an appropriate selection of these a sort of inner citadel to which we can retreat when threatened. Once safely inside it, we can look out and feel safer. How can we be so bad, or stupid, or ineffective as we might half feel or by projection suspect that others think we are, if all those good and important things are ours? This belonging-identity becomes, in fact, the most important thing which belongs to us. We spring most eagerly and violently to its defence if anything happens to jeopardize it. If, for example, our husband or wife is unfaithful, our dog is more affable to a casual visitor than to us, our choicest painting turns out to be a fake, our child becomes a hippie, or our new book is exposed as pendantic pomposity, we are not just saddened or angered; we are frightened because part of the identity protecting us from our inability to cope with ourselves has been damaged. We are driven to more desperate lengths and more complex psychological subterfuges than the objective cause would appear to warrant.

We all, to a greater or lesser extent, possess a belonging-identity because our awareness is less than complete. But when awareness rises, belonging-identity becomes weaker. If this happens, as is

49

happening today to so many young people, there is a stage of anxiety and uncertainty because the belonging-identity, however hampering to mature development, provides stabilizing reference points, concrete things we can hang on to. It successfully shows us where we are, but if increasing awareness discredits the pretensions of the belonging-identity it does not yet provide a substitute self-image. This comes only later when increasingly high levels of awareness permit us to develop a sense of self based on what that awareness reveals of our own nature. I have termed this awareness-identity; it is the goal towards which all efforts to increase awareness should be consciously directed.

As I have suggested, the teacher with a low awareness is likely to put all sorts of psychological pressures on his students; if he is strong, they may well be damaged, if weak they will at least lack an inspiring example and at worst learn to despise the adult model. To the extent that he has also a powerful belonging-identity, he will be materialistic, competitive, and conservative.

Materialistic, because his self-assessment is based on things: the things may include qualities such as good taste or sensitivity, but they are derived from what is outside himself ('If I read such sophisticated books, I must have good taste; if I am so moved by tales of suffering, I must be sensitive.') rather than from his real nature which, as his friends could tell him, might be quite different. Hence there would be a falsity about his judgements. He would place a high value on the things that were important in the construction of his own identity, but might have little extrinsic worth. He might, it is true, glory in his association with a rich cultural or social tradition and speak of it with inspiration (as might the Winton teacher). He might equally value some odd personal quirk, the fact that he was white, the fact that he was richer than his neighbours, his membership of a bigoted social or religious movement. These identities may be splendid or they may be mean; what they have in common is that they are psychological artifacts which do not represent reality. (I should emphasize at this point that many of the things which may be components of belonging-identity – such as artistic taste or membership of a community or family – are in themselves good and desirable. They are only bad when incorporated into a structure which may involve manipulation or exploitation of others.)

Competitive, because if we evaluate ourselves by externals we are measuring ourselves against others and, by the same token, are driven to acquire more of the possessions, honours, or qualities that constitute our principal standard of measurement, in order to demonstrate our superiority. In some instances the competitive teacher will actually compete against his students, eager to prove to himself that he is stronger or cleverer than they. In general he will assume the importance of competition as a stimulus and will goad his students to vie with one another.

Conservative, because change implies a threat to the belonging-identity. This may, of course, be enhanced by changes, such as promotion or new dignities, which help us to view ourselves in a brighter light. But any change which invalidates the identity or a key aspect of it is resisted and feared. One reason why some people refuse psychotherapy is because it might reveal features of their personality which contradict their self-image. Belonging-identity is often woven around an individual's involvement with social organizations, churches, traditions, schools of thought, political parties and so on. The use he makes of these for identity purposes may easily be out of harmony with the character of the institution concerned – who has not known the zealous churchman whose way of life is notoriously censorious and unloving? The point of this context is, however, that changes in the institution are rejected as a threat to the identity which makes use of it. Professed revolutionaries can also be conservative in this sense. The very core of their identity may be involved in belonging to a revolutionary group. In this case, their conservatism does not, of course, extend to the society they wish to destroy, but to the structure and ideology of the revolutionary movement which must, at all costs, be preserved. This type of conservatism spreads cancerously through a man's life. The teacher will be reluctant to try new methods, he will only be able to understand or tolerate aspects of excellence which correspond to his own. He will be afraid of originality in his students, he will be aggressively sure of his opinions – woe to the child whose mind is cast in a different mould.

I have elaborated upon the question of the teacher's self-image, his level of awareness and sense of identity, because these things determine his capacity to teach his students in such a way that they too are helped in developing high awareness. A teacher with low awareness, as I have tried to describe him, may of course alienate his students, but whether they like him or not he presents a mode of behaviour which, in the absence of a strong alternative, they may easily adopt; they will in time be tinged with his conservatism and his competitive materialism, suitable servants of the system and the exploitative network. The teacher with high awareness will have the opposite effect. She will help to liberate her students from the fetters of the system so that they may become architects of a peaceful society.

It is one thing, however, to say that teachers should have high awareness so that they in turn can promote it among their students, and quite another to prescribe for its achievement. The first step, perhaps, is to recognize how little we have and to watch for the effect which low awareness may have upon our behaviour, particularly, if we are teachers, in the classroom. The very fact of this observation activates the more aware aspect of ourselves, the awareness-identity, and this may lead us to different practices and attitudes which will become increasingly habitual.

In this chapter I have tried to indicate the factors present in all of us which militate against our capacity to teach in such a manner as to promote a peaceful society. To recognize them may be in part to overcome them, but there are in addition specific approaches to teaching which may positively help us to educate for liberation.

5
Affective Education

At this point I must take a side step to examine briefly and inadequately the vast, incoherent, and overlapping fields of work known as affective education, psychological education, humanistic education, fulfilment education, education of concerns, and a number of other comparable terms.[4] This is education which recognizes as its conscious goals, as Paul Nash (1971) puts it, the education of feelings and actions as well as thinking, education which is in fact affective or behavioural rather than solely intellectual. No education is, of course, purely intellectual; on the contrary, much of it has a devastating emotional impact, but this is a side effect, not consciously planned, of cognitive education. It has this effect because, the exponents of affective, etc., education would say, it only takes into account part of the human being.

It is, naturally, no new idea that education should do more than train the intellect. The English public schools, under the inspiration of Dr Arnold, aimed to produce God-fearing and loyal Christian gentlemen, while much further back Spartan schooling was an education in stoic courage. Recently, however, there has been a spate of writing on new ways in education. Much of it is clustered around two centres. One is represented by a group of men and women, mostly teachers, many young, who are angered by the mindlessness, the dehumanizing quality, the subtly obnoxious hidden curriculum, and the intellectually

[4] The most comprehensive description of this rather vague field that I know of is in Lyon (1971). I am equally indebted to the shorter, but more critical assessment by Deborah Ramsey (1971).

worthless education prevailing in the schools for failure and most of Xville High. They have attempted to discover ways in which education can be made more real, more interesting, more exciting, even in one case, more ecstatic. This movement has exposed many evils, made useful propaganda, and from time to time produced extremely valuable teaching manuals. Outstanding among, but representative of, these are Kohl's *The Open Classroom: A Practical Guide to a New Type of Teaching* (1969) and Terry Borton's *Reach, Touch and Teach* (1970). Their approach to the process of education in humane, intelligent, and deft. They do not ignore the intellectual aspect; on the contrary, as their examples show, their students make great progress in their capacity to write with creativity and feeling, to analyse problems, to make mature judgements, and to appreciate music or literature. This is only possible, however, because the teacher values them as individuals and creates a social setting (primarily a relationship with them) in which they are not made to feel stupid or inferior, in which they are not subjected to pointless and humiliating regulations, and in which their interests and capacities – untouched by rough impersonal instruction – are delicately uncovered and stimulated.

So far so good. The important question for me is how far excellent teaching of this sort will contribute towards achieving the objectives I have set for education: the raising of awareness, the reduction of competitive materialism, and the establishment of a peaceful society. This sort of teaching I take to be the pedagogical groundwork for these other developments. Unless children in school are released from fear, the sense of failure, and the prevalent meaningless futility, they will be stunted both intellectually and emotionally, and incapable of tackling the formidable tasks of social transformation – the peaceful society will not be born without pain and effort.

On the other hand, what the fortunate pupils of Kohl or Borton are experiencing is not new to the boys at Winton, who have high intellectual competence, interests and abilities which are stimulated and developed, and are emotionally secure. How far this results from their education and how far from the fortunate circumstances of their birth and background it is hard to say, but it is reasonable to suppose at least that the latter are reinforced by the former. It is certainly true that in almost equally aristocratic but less educationally-advanced schools there is less versatile virtuosity on the scholastic side while socially there is the same sense of superiority, but more narrow and intolerant.

What is lacking is awareness. True, the feelings are released from constricting cocoons of convention, prejudice, and fear of seeming 'weak', 'soft' or 'odd'. This is certainly a step forward, but strong feelings can be as blinding as lack of affect – or indeed, as an ill-disciplined or illogical intellect. Awareness, as I have tried to define it, is the total sense of self that lies behind the often distracting activities of mind and emotion. Intellectual activity refined to the point where it spins out ideas about ideas about ideas (as, for example, in some literary criticism) is of no help in tackling the intellectual problems of living effectively, let alone the emotional ones. Emotions, the marvellous capacity to love each other and to experience wonder, joy and mirth, compassion and grief, can also be readily transmuted into fear, self-pity, jealousy, depression, anxiety, anger, envy and a dozen other debilitating forms which sap the energy which we need to achieve our evolution. Someone whose emotions are 'educated' can merely be a person who allows his feeling to bubble to the surface, whether they are constructive and positive, or what has been termed negative emotions. One might argue that the more expression of feelings is inhibited, the more likely they are in fact to be negative.[5] But this is in any case a very normal tendency. A few minutes of introspection will reveal how little control we have over the flow of our emotions. They flicker across the screen of consciousness or semi-consciousness, touching chords of association, bringing now a moment of self-satisfaction; now a vaguely unpleasant feeling which – should we catch and pin it to the dissecting board – will turn out to be a sense of

[5] I take this term from Ouspensky (1949). Negative emotions are those which, like jealousy, anxiety, self-pity, or irritation, leave us feeling weakened. They drain away some form of psychic energy and leave us less capable of creativity, of empathy, or purposeful activity.

guilt or inadequacy; now calmness, now anxiety, now elation, now a minor, unidentified depression. The pure emotions, those which are based upon direct perception or relationship rather than fantasy, and which do not leave us with a slight feeling of enervation, easily become corroded. Suppose, for example, that we are genuinely moved to compassion by a friend's adversity; almost at once, however, we begin to feel smugness that the disaster did not happen to us, fear lest it might, and self-satisfaction that we are so sensitive to another's misfortune: the flavour of the original emotion will long since have disappeared.

To be aware is to be in touch with what lies behind our thoughts and feelings, the self from which they originate and which they serve, but often badly. The education of the servants is not education of the self, though if the servants are strong and disciplined the self will be more powerful.

The second group of persons, inevitably overlapping in ideology considerably with the first, whose writings are directly or indirectly relevant to education, are psychologists and psychiatrists. These belong to the loose-knit school which includes Alport (1957), Fromm (1956), Maslow (1968), Perls (1969), and Rogers (1961 and 1969). They are related by their general belief in the possibility of man's self-realization, self-actualization, his possibility of regeneration through peak experiences, or whatever comparable terminology they employ. Unlike an older, and indeed current psychological generation, they hold in common that man is not an essentially bad and destructive creature who is only held in check by social conditioning, but that he has sublime potentialities. It is the work of the therapists and the teachers to supply first the conditions in which these potentialities can develop, and secondly the stimulus for them to do so.

In their examination of man's possible modes of development, they bring into the realm of psychology what was previously in the realm of religion. It is unimportant that some of these psychologists have apparently not believed in a god who created the universe for particular purposes (Maslow), while others apparently did (Allport). What does matter is that for the first time since William James (1902)[6] a reputable body of psychologists has considered that religious experience is a legitimate field for inquiry – Fromm (1960) actually collaborated on a book on Zen – and so have elected to study a range of phenomena which most of their predecessors had considered to be fanciful or irrelevant, or the symptoms of neurosis.

If these phenomena could be captured in a single phrase, one might perhaps speak of expanded consciousness. Traditionally the task of psychology has been to discover principles of mental function, of perception, cognition, motivation and the like. This meant to establish norms, to discover statistical validities, to systematize data. Thus we develop concepts of average behaviour which we tend to view as normal, natural, or healthy behaviour. But mystical experiences are not normal, in the sense that few people have them very often. They do not fit into the psychological system except as aberrations. What Maslow, Allport and others have done, however, is to affirm that they are not only part of the system, but the most important part. Not only are they far from being aberrations, but they represent man's optimum condition and functioning, and should be striven for. An expanded consciousness is neither a fantasy nor a sickness, but a potentiality realized. Moreover, it may be a relatively common part of our existence – 'The sacred is *in* the ordinary,' says Maslow (1970, p. x), but we fail to recognize it because we are trained to distrust and apologize for these apparently aberrant types of feeling.

I can perhaps best convey their flavour by quoting Maslow (1970, pp. 61–3) on what he terms peak experiences.

'In the peak experiences, we become more detached, more objective, and are more able to perceive the world as if it were independent not only of the perceiver but even of human beings in general. The perceiver can more readily look upon nature as if it were there in itself and for itself, not simply as if it were a human playground put there for human purposes.

[6] This great work is an indispensable source for all who are dissatisfied with conservative psychiatric interpretations of human nature.

He can more easily refrain from projecting human purposes upon it. In a word, we can see it in its own Being (as an end in itself) rather than as something to be used or something to be afraid of or something to wish for or to be reacted to in some other personal, human, self-centred way. . . . This is a little like talking about god-like perception, super-human perception. The peak experience seems to lift us to greater than normal heights so that we can see and perceive in a higher than usual way. We become larger, greater, stronger, higher, taller people and tend to perceive accordingly. . . . To say this in a different way, perception in the peak experiences can be relatively ego-transcending, self-forgetful, egoless, unselfish. It can come closer to being unmotivated, impersonal, desireless, detached, not needing or wishing. . . . In the peak experience there is a very characteristic disorientation in time and space, or even the lack of consciousness of time and space. Phrased positively, this is like experiencing universality and eternity. . . . The person in the peak experience may feel a day passing as if it were minutes, or also a minute so intensely lived that it might feel like a day or a year or an eternity even. He may also lose his consciousness of being located in a particular place. . . . The world seen in the peak experience is seen only as beautiful, good, desirable, worthwhile, etc., and is never experienced as evil or undesirable. The world is accepted. People will say that then they understand it. Most important of all for comparison with religious thinking is that somehow they become reconciled to evil. Evil itself is accepted and understood and seen in its proper place in the whole, as belonging there, as unavoidable, as necessary and, therefore, proper.'

In the beginning of the section from which these quotations were taken, Maslow says (p. 59), 'practically everything that happens in the peak experiences, naturalistic though they are, could be listed under the headings of religious happenings, or indeed have been in the past considered to be only religious experiences.' There is little to differentiate the peak experiences from what Rudolph Otto (1958) has defined as the characteristics of religious experiences: sense of veneration, of awe, of worship, of smallness before mystery, of sublime exaltation, of the power-lessness of the individual, of the unity of creation, of the desire to kneel in worship. Maslow believes that these sensibilities de-rive from heeding the delicate voices of our own central inner humanness; the deist would maintain that they came from God. It seems to me unnecessary to argue which is right.

In my *Militants and Mystics* (1972) I attempt to elaborate a theory of awareness and identity and to relate these two things to social action. As the general level of awareness rises, that is to say, as individuals become increasingly conscious of themselves, they also become increasingly conscious of what is around them-selves. The consciousness is, moreover, the full awareness which includes as an inescapable component the need to act upon it. I have found that the type, rather than the level, of heightened awareness, differs. It may on the one hand be what I term natural or self-consciousness, that is to say spontaneous or achieved pur-posely, as through therapy, T-groups and the like, or it may be supraliminal. By supraliminal I mean what might otherwise be called consciousness-expanding or mystical; it is achieved less by psycho-analysis or sensitivity training than by the practice of Zen, yoga, or indeed many other cults or religions (or rather people *attempt* to reach it by these means: whether they succeed and in what degree and whether the results differ from others more orthodox is a matter for speculation). On the whole, natural or self-conscious awareness tends to be more prosaic, to represent the well-functioning mind uncluttered by anxieties and pre-judices; supraliminal awareness (to the extent that it is achieved) has more the spiritual quality of Maslow's peak experiences. There is, of course, considerable overlap, but those whose mode of awareness tends to be more natural than supraliminal are likely to be militant in their social action. That is to say, their approach to social evils is to eradicate them by changing the institutions which produce them. On the other hand, those whose awareness is supraliminal rather than natural feel that the insti-tutions are evil and that they themselves are also in part respons-ible for this evil. Moreover, if what was bad is to become good through their agency, it is first necessary for them to perfect themselves. Whereas the militant and the mystic both wish to change society, the former tries to do so by direct intervention, the latter through self-purification.

At a higher level of development, the mystic and the militant modes merge in the persons of such men as Gandhi. I believe that this coming together of the outward and inward activist is of supreme importance in moving society towards peace. Institutions may certainly be changed through many types of revolutionary action, but without the mystical element the old ills are likely to recur under any new dispensation. Unless the actors are relatively free of negative emotion, and the particular manifestations of it associated with the belonging-identity and competitive materialism, fresh institutional arrangements alone cannot afford protection against rapacity and exploitation. And without militant action of some sort the spiritual evolution of the mystics is not able to bring about the material changes necessary to peace.

My concept of awareness includes as an inseparable element the sense of social involvement, sensitivity to social injustice, empathy with suffering, and in general the capacity to relate warmly to other people. This, I believe, is not inconsistent with what Maslow, Fromm, and others are saying. (In the Appendix, I compare my approach to that of a different type of psychologist – B. F. Skinner.) I may simply be outlining aspects of the situation which, because of my basic concern with peace, is of greater interest to me than to them.

According to Maslow, there is a hierarchy of human needs – the satisfaction of basic bodily wants; safety, including protection, shelter, sufficient income and other forms of security; social needs for companionship and friendship; ego needs for recognition, status and esteem; and only when these have been satisfied come the higher needs for creativity and self-actualization. Thus the good teacher would be one who to the greatest possible extent ensured for the children in his charge the satisfaction of needs up to and including ego needs so that they would be ready to take off on original and exciting learning experiences. I find it hard to follow Maslow fully on this point. Many of the people of high awareness whom I have known could not be neatly categorized as having all their lower wants satisfied; on the contrary, some have been needy persons facing extraordinary difficulties. Maslow makes it sound rather middle class and this is precisely what awareness, as I know it, is not. It is a wandering and erratic flame but one which, once we have sighted it, we long to capture and, in the striving, do in part make our own.

However, I believe that the conditions for satisfying the ego needs correspond to a second vitally important tenet which the psychologists, though in varying degrees of strength and specificity, hold in common. This might be termed belief in the value of freedom. It is significant that Carl Rogers entitles the book in which he applies his psychological understanding to problems of identification, *Freedom to Learn* (1969). What this means, briefly put, is that when human beings are constrained to learn subjects which are uninteresting or unreal and are, moreover, merely passive recipients of instruction (which in fact tends to make most topics boring and void) they not only fail to learn but also to develop in other ways as well. However, when there is some give and take in the learning process, when there is dialogue rather than monologue, when they have some initiative in following their own interests and arranging their own studies, they not only learn more, but also mature as human beings. The encounter group is one technique for breaking down the emotional adhesions created by what Rogers (1969, p. viii) terms, 'the most traditional, conservative, rigid, bureaucratic institution of our time' (namely the educational system) and enabling this freer, happier, and more efficient form of learning to take place.

From our point of view, the right type of freedom in education has two important implications. In the first place it eliminates what is unpeaceful in the relationship of the teacher and the taught, the all too easily intrusive element of exploitation and manipulation. Thus the learning relationship can serve as a good model for relationships in the wider world, one in which understanding, nurturing, and care replace the impassible barriers of

61

hierarchy. Secondly, the process of developing freedom in learning and the flexible relationship on which it depends involves, in various ways, a re-learning of the self. One becomes less of a machine, no longer behaving entirely according to rule, learning to respond to elements in one's surroundings and in one's self which are intrinsic to one's nature. In this one does, in Maslow's terms, experience the gratification of ego needs. I would maintain, however, that our subsequent development does not occur because one is then liberated from these needs, but rather because the process through which incidentally, they are gratified, may be one which increases awareness.

There are, of course, many aspects of affective education upon which I have not touched. Moreover, I fear that in my references to Rogers and especially to Maslow I have, to make my point, given undue emphasis to particular aspects of their rich philosophies. I have perhaps given the impression that they are in one camp, with Borton, Kohl and other teachers in a different one. But of course there is much sharing and cross-fertilization and a common basic conception to lend light, lightness and feeling to education, all too often a dark and heavy factory of frequently meaningless knowledge.

Within the many approaches to affective, etc., education, some separate, many interlocking or overlapping, there is much which is relevant to education for liberation. It certainly provides a part of the foundation upon which the peaceful society must be built. What is lacking, I believe, is a coherent philosophy of the relationship of education to society which would make it possible for the real strength of affective education to be directed towards transforming the social setting which neutralizes so much good contemporary work in education.

6

The Learning Relationship

We are taught both directly and indirectly. My teacher may teach me Spanish, but the manner of his teaching, his attitude and behaviour towards me and his feelings about himself may teach me a whole range of other things. If he is a man of humanity and awareness, I may learn trust and self-confidence, to be intellectually enterprising, and to enjoy my mental processes. If, on the other hand, he is narrow and pompous, unsure of himself and constantly attempting to bolster his faltering ego, or seething with unexpressed rage, he will teach me to be cautious, circumspect, suspicious of moody adults, afraid of my intellectual impulses, conservative and passive: into the bargain I will probably not learn so much Spanish. Teaching, in fact, is far more than the imparting of knowledge; it includes, intentionally or not, the communication of feelings about human relationships, about oneself and one's value and competence, about the whole business of learning, and in general about the way one handles one's life. These feelings may correspond very little to the reality about oneself or others, but their influence may be great. If, for example, a teacher believes that a child is incapable of success, he may take little trouble to try to teach him and will convey his low opinion of him in many subtle ways. The child, in consequence, probably will fail. This works in the opposite way as well. A child in whom the teacher has unreasonable confidence is likely to do well simply because of that confidence.

A teacher, then, is much more than someone who pours forth knowledge out of himself into another. In one sense he shapes the vessel into which this knowledge is poured, but this metaphor, though neat, omits an important part of the truth. It is not only the teacher who teaches the student, but the student who teaches himself. Most of what you and I know we have taught ourselves. This is a good thing too, because if we had relied on what we learned in school and university, we should, since knowledge is expanding exponentially, be sadly out of date even if we remembered it, which I for one do not. What the teacher can and should do is to stimulate our intellectual curiosity, impart sound judgement, teach us to think logically, give us a measure of balanced confidence in ourselves, in short be what Rogers (1969, pp. 157–66) calls a facilitator of learning. Nor is this the whole story, for if learning in the most complete sense is to occur, it must be reciprocal, the teacher and the student must share and exchange their knowledge, teaching each other. They must, in fact, be open to each other and the teacher must be sufficiently aware to accept gratefully what he has to learn from the student.

A teaching situation which has all these attributes will be one which establishes the prerequisites for the growth of awareness. Despite all good intentions, a teacher's own inner complexities, his irritations, anxieties, prejudices, his fragile self-esteem, are likely to get in the way of his relationship with his student. Not only will these things cloud his vision so that he sees the student through a haze of annoyance or worry, but they will impel him to use the relationship to obtain some relief; he will, for example, seek to dominate the student, thus reassuring himself of his own strength, or to bolster his own *amour propre* by inciting his admiration. Or then again he may be so exhausted by coping with these assaults upon his peace of mind that he has little feeling left over to build an emotional bridge between himself and the student. What happens between the teacher and the taught also occurs, of course, between human beings in every situation (which adds a perilous and seldom-acknowledged dimension to world affairs); we manipulate or drain each other to assuage our own inner pains, or have little left over from our self-concern to give to each other. Of course there are many exceptions. People often give more than they take, but it is still rare to find a person who accepts us spontaneously with a completely undemanding warmth.

There is a particular delicacy about the student–teacher relationship. In a sense it is one between the strong and the weak, but it is not mediated by natural affection as is the parent–child relationship. In addition, there is a tradition of hierarchy and these two combined can readily breed oppression. Moreover, it is in this difficult context that the subtle and sensitive process of education has to occur. No wonder that it frequently turns sour.

The teacher's first task is, perhaps, to understand how readily things go wrong because he is absorbed in his own inner difficulties and therefore uses the relationship wrongly. Before meeting students he should come to terms with himself in order to avoid carrying over his own negative emotions into the conversation or teaching. He should try to look at what is disturbing him – which will then certainly at once become less disturbing – and then to become inwardly quiet. Even if he is not conscious of any focus of inner unrest, he would do well to give himself a respite from the flow of feelings and images which normally chase each other across the screen of consciousness.

This would make it much easier for him to accept the students for themselves, as human beings in their own right apart from how they affect him. He should try to *feel* them, to enter into them although, paradoxically, the more he accepts them the more he also recognizes their intrinsic and invaluable yet incomprehensible difference. The more aware we become, the more we recognize the limit of awareness. The more we become aware of others, the more we recognize the unknowable. When we are less aware we see others in terms of their similarities to or differences from ourselves, but greater awareness shows us a glimpse of what cannot be described in these terms and which we therefore cannot grasp. Thus acceptance of others is acceptance of the unintelligible. What we cannot know we cannot judge, and the only attitude we can adopt is one of trust, respect, and interest in helping this unknown person to fulfil her or his potentialities. If we are other than receptive, patient and helpful, these potentialities may never emerge.

65

I can best describe this part of the teacher's role as being actively passive, as listening so intently to another's unspoken thoughts that the noise of her own mind fades into nothing. This, I believe, is the necessary preliminary to saying what should be said, to providing the information to help this other person to solve a problem, whether on the emotional or on the intellectual level.

At the next stage, the teacher has to establish the right relationship with her own knowledge. This is something upon which many teachers pride themselves and the higher the teacher's level – high school more than elementary, college more than high school – the greater the evaluation of that knowledge; after all, as we have seen, more has been paid for it in terms of time and money. Our knowledge is apt to become part of our belonging-identity; it becomes part of the self-image upon which we depend for security, as do our badges of knowledge – degrees, diplomas, publications, honorific appointments, and the like. For this reason, we feel a need to be respected for our knowledge and if it is questioned or shown to be faulty, we suffer and react with self-protective fear, anger, or self-justification. This makes us bad teachers because we are more concerned with protecting our little gobbet of intellectual expertise than with its veracity or accuracy. It may also make us poor scholars if we become so desperate to defend our point of view that we cannot listen to another; on the other hand, we may be compulsively driven to keep ahead of our professional competitors, in which case we become that type of intolerantly brilliant academic who is usually so disliked by his students.

In such cases, knowledge is a commodity, not only for buying a slice of the system, but also for establishing an acceptable self-image. I believe that knowledge serving either of these purposes is antithetical to the aims of education as I have formulated them. The true teacher should not be identified with his own necessarily skewed and limited fragment of information. It should serve as a springboard from which he and his students can leap farther, understand more, and as a result reassess what they thought they knew earlier. In fact knowledge is not a fixed quantity, but a fluid element, impelling us to realize that our previous knowledge was relative and impermanent. Oddly enough, it is easier to recognize this in more advanced studies concerned, for example, with the uncertainties of historical interpretation or nuclear physics. At a much lower level, it would seem that the fundamental facts of, for example, French grammar or arithmetic are inalienable intellectual constructs. But are they? The rules of grammar depend upon linguistic structure and those of arithmetic on concepts of numbers about which more is being learned every year. While the infinitive of to have is *avoir*, the meaning of have and the use of the infinitive is seen in ever-widening perspectives; by the same token, the so-called new mathematics has placed simple addition and multiplication in a much larger numerical context.

Thus the good teacher should not be identified emotionally with his knowledge because it damages his rapport with his students. In addition, it can easily make him a bad scholar, one who is anchored to a set of concepts which no longer represent what is best in his field; valid knowledge, on the other hand, will enable him to leap imaginatively from the security of familiar facts and ideas into a new and uncharted realm.

The teacher who is able to cut loose from his knowledge will teach very differently from the one who cannot. The knowledge of the teacher as opposed to the pure scholar in his library or laboratory, involves much more than simply knowing about a subject. It also involves knowing about young people and how to teach them. Again, this must be a very open sort of knowledge. Its essence is that it has no boundary and no fixed points. The teacher who firmly proclaims 'I know what children are like', and announces inflexible rules of procedure to his class has made this aspect of his knowledge as much a part of his identity as the knowledge he formally teaches.

Does all this imply that a teacher requires no knowledge of his teaching subjects, of child psychology, classroom procedure and the like; that he only needs to be open and flexible? Not in the least. She must be able to lay a reliable foundation of information, to combine stimulation with accuracy and facts with theories, to understand the right pace to move with his class, to appreciate children's intellectual problems and to know how to overcome them.

In my opinion the teacher should approach her class in terms of something like the following. 'We are going together on a journey of exploration. I know parts of the country and you know others; just because you are alive and use your senses and have experienced things which I have not, you know things which I do not know. You may not realize that you know them, but it is my job as a teacher to help you become aware of what you know and to recognize its significance. We shall all learn from each other by sharing what we know. In this way we shall explore together much more of the country than we could have done alone. My responsibility is to make sharing easier and to contribute my own knowledge and experience to the common pool.'

This sort of approach, it might be argued, would do very well with advanced students considering, say, social change or urbanization, but would be quite inappropriate to young children who are being grounded in a basic subject. Here, it is true, the knowledge of a teacher will greatly exceed that of the student, but even in these cases some reciprocity is possible. There is no subject so elementary that the learner cannot contribute actively to his own learning or add something to the teacher's appreciation of what he is teaching. As Whitehead (1959) observed, the subject matter of education, however much we may subdivide it, is 'to represent life as it is known in the midst of living it,' and no human being has a monopoly of wisdom upon that vast subject. The teacher who fails to understand this or to recognize that he too is a learner at once separates himself from his students; and his behaviour towards them will teach them, much more effectively than he is teaching them spelling or addition, that they are inferior beings. Their behaviour will in turn be influenced as much, or more, by the desire to placate the teacher and to avoid trouble and ignominy as by the wish to learn.

Some might maintain that children expect infallibility and that the teacher who admits to fallibility and places himself on the same level as his students, as an explorer, forfeits his authority. This, unfortunately, is true in a certain sense. Some children have been conditioned to an authoritarian adult world with which there can be no dialogue: father knows best; and the teacher knows best; the textbooks are always right. I remember one child saying to me, eyes shining, 'Miss Smith is so brilliant, she knows the whole of the history book by heart.' Her feeling for the teacher was a compound of fear and slavish admiration, which it would be hard to call respect. On the other hand, I have heard students speak with genuine warmth of their teachers because, 'they didn't mind admitting that they were wrong, or that they did not know'. To the extent that we are impressed with the omniscience of the teacher, we learn only what he knows. Whether this is a lot or a little does not matter so much. What is important is that we are not learning to move by ourselves beyond the teacher; and that is the essence of learning. Ultimately the authority of the teacher depends upon his capacity to stimulate this sort of learning and this capacity in turn depends upon his honesty and awareness.

The task of a teacher whose students want to admire him, to sit back passively and receive his knowledge, is not easy. He has to awaken them, to ensure their awareness of their own knowledge, but this often involves exposing himself to their resentment and incredulity. He has to wean them of independence upon the passive acceptance of his domination and lead them towards intellectual and emotional freedom. In this sense, the process of education becomes one of liberation.

These ideas have gradually developed as a result of my own work as a teacher (see also Curle (1971), pp. 158–66) and it may be relevant at this point to become more personal and to describe some of the situations through which, thinking in this way, I have been led. I should explain that most of my teaching has been carried out with graduate students studying such topics as problems of social and educational development in poor countries, conflict and social change, education and society, and social psychology.

From time to time my ideas on these topics have crystallized into a system which I have been very happy to expound. My lectures have been received with a general deference I have found gratifying and I have felt slightly irritated by the criticisms of those who have not swallowed my ideas hook, line and sinker. But systems are made to be broken out of. They represent a temporary fitting together of whatever we know at a given moment of time and should serve primarily as a starting point for moving on. If we cling to the system we do not move on. I am probably a better teacher, a better learning facilitator, in the inter-system phases of my intellectual life. At these times, no longer slightly deluded by the attractive neatness of the system, I am more open, more receptive, I realize that my perception of reality is extremely limited, that my particular expertise can only reveal a fragment of it, and I try to encourage my students to join me in discovering a little more. These students are people of considerable and diverse talents and experience; I tell them that if their insights can be recognized and shared we shall all be the wiser. There are, however, always some individuals who suggest that this is the wrong way to proceed; they have come to me because I have a reputation in the field and they want to hear what I have to say. My answer is that I shall certainly share with them anything I know which is appropriate to the theme of the class, but not in the form of lectures delivered *ex cathedra*, to be accepted because it is I who have pronounced them.

My usual procedure is, in fact, to start the ball rolling with a few more formal statements which set the stage and give the students time to do some basic reading and to adjust their minds to the matters in question. I also ask them to think about presentations, based on experience or reading, which they might themselves make to the class. Within a few weeks I begin to take an increasingly back place. At first I act more or less formally as chairman to the student or group of students who are presenting a topic for consideration and discussion; later, depending somewhat on the composition of the class, my role becomes almost indistinguishable from that of student members. I may talk a good deal if I feel I have something to contribute, or very little.

Often I am simply learning and have nothing to say. The class at this stage begins to take corporate responsibility for itself, making decisions, in which I may or not have a part, about topics to cover and who should report on what to the class.

Of course things do not always work out as I would wish. Some of the topics, race, for example, are explosive. There are angry confrontations, emotional 'non-academic' discussions, and conflicts develop which may not readily be resolved. This can be painful, difficult and in some cases unsatisfactory. On the other hand, upon looking back, I see that from these sessions that I have learned most in a three-dimensional sense about the meaning of oppression, prejudice, and racism. Then again, some individuals are clearly ill at ease in this type of learning situation. I try to explain in advance how I expect the work of the class will unfold, so that anyone who feels uncomfortable with this approach can register for an alternative class, but there are perhaps always a few who come expecting to profit from it, and find they do not. It is sometimes possible to help these people, to bring them into the work of the group without threatening their security, but this depends upon circumstances, particularly the size of the seminar. The ideal size for such a group is perhaps fifteen, which combines a sufficient diversity with intimacy: mine are often perforce larger. But it is not easy to know how people are responding. I have sometimes been worried about individuals who sat silently through session after session for weeks on end, but many of those eventually found their place in the group and made valuable contributions: they were slow starters and strong finishers.

Sceptical colleagues have objected that we no doubt have entertaining discussions, but that serious, scholarly work does not get done. One justification for this criticism is that there are no specific requirements for the completion of the course. What I ask is that everyone should contribute to the process of mutual teaching and reciprocal learning. They do this by taking part in discussions, by making presentations and – for those who find it helpful to set out their ideas systematically – by writing papers (but I believe the conventional paper written as a formal obligation is frequently a waste of time). Nor do I set tests or examinations. In consequence, if anyone wishes to free-wheel through the class there is nothing to stop him except his own sense of wasted opportunity. I am not prepared to set what I believe to be unnecessary and even penal conditions in order to prevent a small number of people from misusing their time. In my experience, however, work of high quality is carried out by the great majority of members of the class. In most cases they are intellectually aroused and collaborate vigorously and meticulously in preparing their presentation or following up topics in which they have become interested. Some students have told me that they have done much more work in these conditions of relative freedom than when the requirements are more specific and formal. In these cases, there is a tendency, no doubt reprehensible, to do little more than is needed to get by; this is the academic game in which all too often the teacher's objective is to maintain his position, and the student's is either to outwit or to satisfy the teacher (thus buying his share of knowledge), rather than to learn.

The issue of academic standards is closely associated with that of marking or grading. I do not give grades, except when a student needs one for a specific purpose which – given the exigencies of the system as it now is – must be considered valid, and then I always give a very good one. But regular marking is entirely inconsistent with the equal relationship of shared learning I have been attempting to establish. If I were to separate myself from collaborators and judge them, it would constitute a blatant contradiction of everything I had tried to stand for. How could they then believe my protestations about the value of their own experience and the limitations of my own, and about the necessity for participation in the process of learning? They would appear as a deceitful ruse on the part of the academic top dog, another technique of oppression. The only grading which I consider not only to be acceptable but also, in some respects, educationally valuable, is done by the students themselves. The honest effort to assess the quality of one's intellectual efforts and contribution to group learning can be a help towards awareness.

But such an evaluation can be made, and made more comprehensively, without the student committing himself to a grade, a mark both artificial and arbitrary (as everyone who has awarded grades must acknowledge), having little predictive value for ultimate success, but which nevertheless remains a permanent part of the record. Students do, of course, from time to time fail to learn. This is often the teacher's fault, or the cumulative fault of bad teaching by many inadequate practitioners. But failure to learn should not constitute failure in a course. When students do badly they should be helped to do better and not labelled as failures: a more effective device might be to dock the teacher's salary for the failure of his students. In those rare cases where there is an irreconcilable antipathy between the student and the particular field of learning, he should still not be failed but directed towards more appropriate work. The most foolish system I know demands that if a student gets low grades in one subject, he must get high grades in another if he is to pass; thus for example, a C in English literature must be balanced by an A in chemistry. However, if English literature (as might easily be argued) is an essential part of education, defects in this area will not be compensated for by knowing more chemistry. If, on the other hand, the aim of schooling is not to provide education but a qualification enabling us to take our place in the system, such rules are no more educationally irrational than the rest of what takes place in the schools.

I have sometimes been asked whether my classes are not disguised sensitivity training groups. They are not. There is sometimes, I hope, a degree of interpersonal rapport, and openness to feeling, and a slowly-developing corporate sense which are perhaps unusual in formal classes. There is seldom, however, the personal challenge and probing which characterize sensitivity training. This can, it is true, lead to valuable personal insights, but it cannot readily be combined with intellectual exploration which is not necessarily of a subjective character. It can, moreover, very easily go wrong. I am far from being against sensitivity training as part of the total academic experience, but not as a means of grappling with a particular realm of knowledge.

The approach to the learning relationship which I have tried to outline has several implications for education for liberation: a growth of awareness and comparable weakening of the identity of belonging, and a diminution of competitive materialism with a corresponding detachment from the exploitative network.

Firstly and obviously the absence of grading will remove one aspect, though not I believe a very strong one, of competition. Students will not be trying to please the teacher or to gratify themselves, nor to shine before their friends. They may of course try to do these things in other ways, by talking a great deal in class, or preparing bibliographies, or busily making and distributing summaries of previous sessions, but the total atmosphere – not just the absence of marks – is uncompetitive. It is not easy to be competitive about sharing one's knowledge and experience, about being part of a corporate effort. Moreover, the sort of understanding which develops in this way is, so far as possible, real understanding, the fusion of many viewpoints and experiences, something more rounded and whole than what is learned in most classrooms. It inevitably includes, in many contexts, insight into injustice or oppression and empathy for those who suffer from them. In this sense it is antithetical to competitive materialism and the exploitative network through which it derives psychological nourishment. To this extent it also promotes awareness, because – to approach the issue backwards – empathy indicates some awareness of self. In this case a certain awareness of self has developed through a situation in which people are helped to recognize the validity of their own experience and hence of the self which experiences. There is thus a coincidence between deeper knowledge, less competition, and a weaker belonging-identity for this is fed by the fruits of competitive materialism.

I began to try to teach according to these principles because I hoped that it was the best way of increasing understanding. I continue because I believe that it contributes towards the establishment of a peaceful world. But the flaw is that this takes place within an institution which, like virtually all others, prepares people to work within the system – and in this case at a rather high level. Successful attendance at one of my courses contributes to a qualification which could help students to obtain positions of importance within the system. I hope, of course, that it will encourage them – I use the word advisedly – to oppose the system and to promote the counter-system, but I fear that until education and work preparation are severed, the majority of human beings, however idealistic in youth, will eventually succumb to pressure to use their education as a qualification to enter and serve the system. For this reason we shall shortly consider a necessary corollary to the learning relationship here described. This, as opposed to an approach which can be applied to any subject matter, is an actual curriculum devoted to teaching techniques of non-violent social change.

A NOTE ON TEACHER EDUCATION

Of all types of education the training of teachers is perhaps the worst. In the average institution prospective teachers are stuffed with irrelevant and outdated materials on educational psychology (largely the quantitative aspects of testing, little to do with children) and the history, organization and philosophy of education. Most of this is crammed during the few weeks before and forgotten a few weeks after the qualifying examinations. They are also taught how to teach a particular range of subjects and how to handle a class. This usually involves practical work under the supervision of an experienced teacher and if he is skilful and humane, this aspect of teacher training can be the most useful. All too often, however, the student teacher merely learns how to control spontaneity, crush initiative, instil fear or contempt, enforce passivity, impose meaningless regulations and senseless standards, and to reduce to mindlessness the whole process of education – the process which should be so exciting and enthralling. They have been trapped in the system, initiated and indoctrinated before ever realizing that there was anything else. Many of them go on to teach in Xville High, where a number of their students will, in turn, become teachers while the others become the system-supporting parents of a new but all too similar generation. And so the vicious cycle revolves.

This sort of training does little to prepare people for the type of teaching I have described. On the contrary, to the extent that it has any impact, it deadens and stultifies. I must add, however, that some young people are too wise to be ensnared. To them, their training is simply a waste of time, an unfortunately necessary sacrifice in obtaining the licence to teach, which they believe to be an intrinsically valuable activity. Even today, within the clutches of the system, much can be and in some places is being done to train teachers for liberation.

In the first place there is a new type of person becoming interested in education. They are not so much attracted to conventional careers in education as to the chance of experimenting with new approaches, of putting right some of the things which are so manifestly wrong, of using education as a means for transforming society. Many of these are older people, women with grown children, people with half a career successfully completed who now seek greater personal involvement, members of minority groups who have been serving their people in freedom schools or community organizations, men and women who believe that education could change the world. Many of these are considerably more mature, in experience if not in age, than the average teacher in training. They correspond, at least in part, to the wise human beings who, in my ideal system, would be chosen for the high post of teacher. Teacher-training institutions should encourage applications from such people and seek ways of making the most effective use of their varied backgrounds and knowledge. Many of the formal requirements could be waived, because only those persons should be chosen who had shown in their lives that they could work with strength, sensitivity and persistence.

Much teacher education is marred, because the teachers in training are treated as students at all levels are commonly treated, as irresponsible and inferior beings who must be carefully watched lest they take advantage of their instructors by cheating or lapsing into sloth. At one stage in my career I took charge of a teacher-training institution where I found that there was an extraordinary degree of impersonal regimentation – lectures were compulsory and registers of attendance were kept, there was little contact between the faculty and the students, instruction was by lectures only there being no seminars or discussions, there was a comprehensive final examination on topics which appeared to me to be very far from relevant to the work of an educator, and in general the students were treated as inferior and senseless beings. This sort of system, which is remarkably widespread, seems to be the worst possible form of preparation for teachers. A teacher should be above all things autonomous and aware. He should have made the transition from the dependence which characterizes, however wrongly, the status of the taught to the independence of the teacher. Ideally teacher training should constitute a sort of *rite de passage* during which the taught is transformed into the teacher. But if the subservience of the student teacher is prolonged throughout his training period, it is far harder for him to reverse his role and he is likely to perpetuate in his own teaching the authoritarian forms of relationship that he has himself experienced.

The relationship between instructors and teachers in the context of teacher training should primarily be that of colleagues, equally concerned with problems of children and their education. The implication of this for the actual training is, it seems to me, considerable. The students should be treated as responsible adults, capable of making their own decisions. They should be trusted to do what was necessary to increase their competence as teachers and not watched, registered and reported on. Lest this degree of freedom deteriorate into misdirected confusion, it would be essential for the embryo teachers to have close relationships with advisers, with whom they could readily discuss all aspects of their programmes whenever they wished. The mutuality of this relationship would be very different from the one-way relationship, from the top downwards, which is prevalent. This type of relationship should help the students eventually to teach in the manner discussed in this chapter.

Another needed reform in many teacher-training institutions

is the curriculum. The unappetizing gobbets of educational psychology, educational theory and the like have little relationship to teaching. Even when interestingly taught by capable instructors, they are remote from the realities of children and classrooms. I believe that the curriculum should be divided into halves. The first should be wholly directed towards developing competence in teaching. There would be much practical work under skilled master teachers, followed by discussion between the master teachers and the student teachers about the methods used, the successes and failures, and the methods of further developing the subjects taught. What psychology was taught would relate to the practice. Psychological theories as such would not be taught in the abstract. Instead, the classroom experiences of the student teachers would be discussed and analysed, and as more general principles of learning or behaviour seemed to be emerging, comparisons would then be made with the relevant work of, say, Piaget or Freud.

The second half of the curriculum would be the study of the wider context of education, of the social and the individual problems which converged on the process of education. These would include, in various settings, issues of peace, of race, of poverty, of the relationship of individuals to social situations, and indeed of many of the issues discussed in these pages. This would not only help teachers to view their task in the widest possible perspective, but to heighten their personal awareness.

A period of training based upon such general principles could have the ultimate result of enabling teachers to view their students as human beings, not as some different and probably dangerous sort of animal. I used at one stage to teach a special class in a predominantly black area of Boston. At the end of the afternoon the children had to file out of their rooms in a certain order, at a particular speed, by a particular route; the teacher stood in the corridors shouting instructions, 'Slow down, that row; hurry up, you; don't get ahead of the others; don't talk; keep near the wall' and so on. The teachers were tensely white-lipped and I was inescapably reminded of circus performers in a cage of tigers, cracking their whips and issuing sullenly-obeyed commands, but fearing that if they hesitated or stopped ranting the animals would tear them to pieces. That human beings should feel about and behave towards other human beings in this way is a serious indictment of the way in which teachers are prepared and of the setting in which they are subsequently called on to function.

This topic is discussed at greater length and more specifically in the second part of Chapter 8.

7
Teaching Non-violent Techniques of Social Change

In this chapter we shall be more concerned with what to teach than with how to teach it. This book is the third in a series written around the theme of peace; and peace, as I use the word, means the eradication of violence through which damage is done to our potentiality for becoming what we have it in us to become. This violence can be the physical violence of killing, maiming, or starving, which most effectively destroys or reduces human potential. Or it can be economic, psychological or social. We may be warped or deprived intellectually or emotionally, or we may be prevented from receiving an adequate education because we are involved in a relationship which, on large scale or small, in manipulative, exploitative, oppressive or authoritarian.

If a more peaceful society is to develop (there is probably no such thing as a completely peaceful society; wherever there are human beings they are apt to impose themselves harmfully upon each other), changes must be brought about in social and economic structures which perpetuate those inequalities and injustices which are in essence violent. An education which aims to promote peace must therefore contribute towards changing those structures, not only through the attitudes of mind it generates, but also through the actual knowledge and skills which it inculcates. Education for liberation must, in fact, include instruction in the techniques for creating social change, for building the counter-system.

Broadly speaking, there are two ways to bring about social change, the violent and the non-violent. I discussed these alternatives in *Making Peace* and was drawn to the non-violent position, though I am bound to admit that violence may under some circumstances appear to be the only solution to intolerable situations. For example, the armed intervention of India was almost certainly necessary to bring to an end the miseries inflicted by Pakistani oppression in Bangladesh; Gandhi himself said that violence was preferable to cowardice. But it seems to me that in general, though violence may tear down a particular oppressor, it does not necessarily get rid of oppression. All too often where an oppressive regime has been overthrown its revolutionary successor has perpetuated the same offences against his own opponents, including the former rulers; all that has occurred is a reversal of roles. There seems, moreover, to be a fundamental psychological inconsistency in the idea of opposing violence by the methods of the violent; if one does so, there is great danger that the seeds of violence within one will take deep root and that oppression may come to appear as a wholly acceptable tool for perpetuating the regime by which the earlier oppression has been replaced. In this sense violence may simply lead to results which benefit one group previously subjected to it, but may not change the total balance of human well-being.

Sometimes, of course, oppressors preach a non-violent philosophy to the oppressed, while continuing to practise violence upon them. This, it need hardly be said, is not the sense in which I advocate non-violence. To do violence is to damage another individual's potential for growth and this may be done by harming him physically, by exploiting him economically, by oppressing him politically, manipulating him emotionally – or by making him weak and submissive when he should be strong and militant. Thus the oppressors who by advocating non-violence to the oppressed are encouraging passivity and are in fact doing subtle violence to them.

To my mind, non-violence is a technique of resistance; it has nothing to do with submission. It is not a resigned rejection of retaliation, but an active and tough-minded assault upon abuses and injustices, but it is one (when practised by such as Gandhi) which recognizes that the oppressor is also human; it aims to oppose, thwart and overcome him without diminishing his humanity. Indeed, as Paulo Freire (1970, ch. 1) points out, the oppressor is as much diminished by his oppression as those upon whom he exercises it. If, therefore, his oppression can be brought to an end without further degrading him, he will ultimately be the gainer. But non-violence is not simply a position to be justified ideologically but by expediency. It may be politically wise because it does not so readily create a vicious backlash on the part of the oppressors; it may win over many who really favour radical change but not violence. It is not so likely to involve counter violence which, since the oppressors are more apt to be strong and well-armed, may be disastrously destructive. It may be less conducive to hatred and the desire for revenge. From our point of view, it might be cynically added, no school is going to teach a curriculum dealing with violent revolution. On the other hand, there is an interest, widely if thinly spread, in ways of teaching non-violent methods of social change.

What follows is simply one man's personal and provisional view of a possible approach to a curriculum on non-violent change. Its object is to stimulate or provoke rather than define. Anyone who wishes to pursue the topic should, of course, read deeply in the writings of and concerning Gandhi (1927), (Fischer 1950), Danilo Dolci (1969) (McNeish 1965), Martin Luther King (King 1969), Albert Luthuli (1962), and other great non-violent activists. He should consult the encyclopaedic work of Gene Sharp (1970 and 1971) as well as the publications of Martin Oppenheimer and George Lakey (1915) and Lakey (1973), practitioners and scholars of social change.

Learning would be concentrated in three main areas:

A. HUMAN NATURE

We can never say that men and women are irredeemably bad. They may perform violent, cruel, selfish, vicious and wanton acts, but every human action results from a combination of what is outside and what is inside a person. Thus the bad behaviour of someone towards myself derives in part (though that part may be very small) from my impact on him or her.

82

Moreover, these bad actions come less from a delight in evil-doing than from fear, ignorance, sickness, or habit. Thus we should not talk collectively of, for example, oppressors (as I admit to doing in this book for the simple sake of convenience), because the people who act oppressively do so from different motives. Some are afraid of losing what they have gained, others believe that another class or race is inferior and should be firmly controlled by those who are better endowed, others are copying their parents, others are possessed by a sense of their impotence and can only achieve a feeling of power by dominating the weak. In some, these motives are deeply ingrained, in others they are superficial. In everyone there are also contradictory elements, tendencies towards gentleness, co-operation, generosity, kindliness, and again in some these are strong even if they are weak in others.

By the same token, if the oppressors are not uniformly evil, the oppressed are not perfect. Many of them, in fact, are also oppressors. Even if they are not in a position to oppress economically or militarily, to be part of an oppressive class or race, there are very few human beings who are not occasionally apt to take advantage of each other, physically, emotionally, socially, or even in a small way financially. However much we struggle outwardly with the manifest forms of oppression, we must also struggle inwardly with the tendencies towards oppression inside ourselves. This, of course, is perfectly manifested in the life and writings of Gandhi. Indeed there may be a close correlation between our capacity to counter external oppression and our conquest in ourselves of the wish to exercise it.

A major lesson to be learned from this is not to indulge in collective thinking, to avoid talking of the oppressors or the enemy (or for that matter of the oppressed) as though they were a single monolithic entity to be overthrown as a whole, completely unamenable to reason or the appeals of morality. The world is made up of people who are mostly rather like ourselves (and this is based on my own experience of living in half a dozen civilizations among people of all estates), whether they are black or white, Christians or Muslims, rich or poor, top dogs or bottom dogs. We have to recognize both the diversity among what appear to be homogeneous groups and the similarity between people of different groups.

To do this is the basis for being able to communicate with each other, or at least for approaching each other with a more positive attitude of mind which may make communication possible.

To recognize these things will also prevent us from doing what in fact makes communication impossible. If we suffer at the hands of people it is difficult for us, if we are given the chance to do so, not to hurt, humiliate, or vilify them. However, while this may give *us* momentary satisfaction, *their* reaction is seldom useful to our long-term objective. They may become angry or resentful, or they may, like some white liberals when blamed by black people for their hidden racism, respond with masochistic confessions of guilt. In neither case, however, has there been a move towards communication, possibly with mutual respect and liking, on which real change in a relationship could be based.

If, on the one hand, we consistently act positively towards the individual, treating him with respect and consideration, while reprobating and opposing his policies, a dual victory may be won – over the oppressive acts or policies, and by the oppressor over his oppressive tendencies. Gandhi's aim was not to humiliate but to uplift his opponents. He wrote (1950, p. 87) that the appeal to the wrongdoer 'is never to his fear; it is, must be, always to his heart'.

Oppression is wrong because it limits the potentiality of human growth and if there is any purpose in human life to which all would subscribe it is perhaps that we should develop to our fullest extent and so make the richest possible contribution to human existence. Oppression is the basis of those unpeaceful relationships with which throughout history the world has been plagued. Apart from the social and material ills to which it so manifestly leads, it has subtle psychological effects. In different ways the oppressive situation dehumanizes both the oppressors and the oppressed.

The member of an oppressed group suffers one of the most extreme and explicit humiliations. Not only will he, probably, be treated with a lack of courtesy and consideration, with condescension or disdain, but he will often feel that, because he is in a position to be thus treated, this is all he deserves. Surely no real man would have allowed himself to sink to such ignominy! He therefore tends to accept the oppressor's evaluation of himself. If they consider him idle, foolish and feckless, then that is what he must be.

In addition, when he has no power or position in his own right, he can only achieve a sense of power and reality by identifying himself with the oppressors. Thus in the Nazis' concentration camps the most dreaded enemies of the average inmates were the privileged prisoners, usually non-political, who had been granted minor positions of authority which they exploited to the hilt. These men would ape the SS guards in every possible way. They would wear, if possible, scraps of their discarded clothing and emulate their swaggering brutality. Thus also in the colonial situation, where the only way to power was the white man's way, many Africans and Asians virtually rejected their own culture to adopt the manners of the colonial rulers. They spoke their language perfectly, played – literally and metaphorically – their games and sought advancement and hence identity through service, albeit in minor capacities, to an alien civilization. But our examples should not all be on so large and formal a scale. Who has not known the child who, because of some lack or defect, is rejected and ridiculed by his peers, but tries to ingratiate himself by imitating their mannerisms? Thus oppression shoves us off centre, preventing our mature development by stress on peripheral tendencies. It impels us to form of a self-mutilation.

It is not only the oppressed, however, who suffer damage. The capacity to oppress in itself indicates some deformity, some less than perfect development. If we know that we are oppressing others, are conscious of what this does to them, yet continue to victimize them, two equally maiming conditions may exist. We may either have no sense of human suffering, which suggests a nadir of awareness, or we may have some empathy but cannot help continuing in our ways, which suggests a nadir of autonomy.

Less extremely, the constant practice of minor oppressions gradually erodes awareness. The self-satisfied paterfamilias, the narrowly arrogant pedant, the school bully, the small bureaucrat whose domestic dissatisfactions are offset by official bombast, and countless other types who thrive upon the servility of those they can dominate, have gradually lost their sensitivity, have become in a sense less than human. In other words, the strength of the belonging-identity has increased and what belongs to them, in this particular context, is the lives or part of the lives of other human beings. To be so dependent on the miseries of others is perhaps the ultimate form of human deprivation.

So both oppressors and oppressed are caught in the same vicious downward spiral. The oppressed, because of their oppression, are the more likely – within the limits of their limited power – to become oppressors and so on *ad infinitum*. Both, also, have latent human qualities. We have, therefore, to fight oppression but to serve and save the oppressors as well as the oppressed. They hold their humanity in common; through their interaction it is diminished. The struggle against oppression will restore both to manhood.

B. SOCIETY

If we are inclined to think too ill of human nature, we tend to think too well of society. Too many of us accept its inequities as part of the scheme of things or, which is worse, to fail to recognize them at all. I recall the farming family who were neighbours when I was a boy. Then they rented land, possessed a dairy herd, and were relatively free, but they had been much poorer. The father had worked as labourer to the squire and he and his wife had reared ten children on a wage of ten shillings (then about $2) a week; it is a miracle that they ever saved enough to buy the cow and pig which started them on the road to partial independence. But even when they had more or less broken the shackles of exploitation they remained affectionately and respectfully loyal to the squire and his family. They would recall with emotion how, in their poorest days ('when I was just a labourer') the squire's wife herself would come around to dispense soup.

I am not criticizing the squire who, as I remember him, was an upright and not unkindly man. He had simply been born into a position of privilege. He owned most of the village and so, in a sense, he owned most of the people. They lived in his houses, they worked on his land, and to some extent he looked after them, but not to the point of giving them a living wage – that would have made him unpopular with his neighbouring landlord friends, would have made the labourers 'greedy' and 'only led to trouble'. Moreover, he could dismiss and evict them at a week's notice if he wanted their cottage for someone else, or if their behaviour displeased him, perhaps because they were suspected of rabbiting on his land to add to their meagre protein ration (rabbits were a pest anyway), or failed to attend church regularly to thank God for His bounty, or had impudent children who failed to give the squire due respect.

Exploitation is an emotive word which we use to stir up popular feelings, but it has a very precise meaning which should be kept in mind when discussing such questions. When I say that the squire exploited his labourers I mean that because he had greater power than they he could impose his will on them to his advantage and their disadvantage. He had land, money and law on his side because he was a magistrate; sitting with him on the bench were others of his kind who would act together to preserve their privileges – or, as they would have put it, to uphold the law. Having these sorts of power he could, and did, use them to his advantage, not because he was cruel, but because people in this position traditionally behaved in this way. He extorted service of a particular kind, long days worked uncomplainingly, obedience and servility in and out of working hours, a 'decent family life and a respectful family', while in return he paid the minimum wage and only did to the cottages what was necessary to prevent structural deterioration. Of course he never saw that he was exploiting his labour-tenants. He would have been most indignant of anyone who had suggested it. He prided himself on his justice and fairness; his village was a happy one, the cottage gardens were well tended, the children clean, the parents knew their place. By helping to create these peaceful conditions he was indeed serving society; the people were content – what more could be desired? Of course many of the people in many of the villages were not content (my old friend was perhaps an exception), but what could they do? They hated and feared the arbitrary authority of the farmer who employed them, but they dared not express their feelings or bargain for better conditions because they lived in tied cottages, and jobs – and hence homes – were hard to get. If they spoke out of turn the landlord would have no hesitation in dismissing them and turning them out of the house, for there would be many eager to take their place.

Things, happily, are now very different in the English countryside. The transformation which has taken place in the first quarter of the century is, indeed, one of the great encouragements to continue working for social change.

The example of exploitation I have just given is a simple and obvious one. There are, however, other sorts of power and other sorts of exploitation. Some of these come, paradoxically, from efforts to overthrow or control the cruder type I have been describing. The labour unions, for example, which enabled farm workers and others (and were perhaps less effective for farm workers than the rest) to stand up without reprisal for their human rights have often themselves become powerful oppressors. They have their own momentum and their own self-image. These often dictate a policy against the interest or conscience of many members who nevertheless must follow the union line or be severely disciplined. Power in communist regimes does not, of course, derive from the accumulation of capital as did the squire's, but from position in the party. The ruling clique acquires privileges and either individually or collectively is as capable of exploitation as any group of capitalists.

We tend to associate power, and hence the capacity to exploit, with wealth. It may be the squire's property which established him as a member of the ruling class for whom the sun rose and the earth turned. Or it may be membership of a powerful group, such as a communist *élite*, controlling the nation's collective wealth, including its armaments. Power is essentially the ability to make the other person worry, to make him think twice before he acts, to make him feel uncomfortable and unsure of himself. The otherwise powerless can exert this sort of power, politically and morally, in various ways which are in effect the techniques of social change and will be discussed in the next section. Eventually by these means the materially weak can overcome the materially strong, which is what happened in India.

The network of oppression and exploitation is infinitely complex and subtle. It is not hard to consider the gross examples involving, say, race or class. It is harder to realize that in virtually every social and economic relationship there is at least a potentiality for these de-humanizing activities. There is always a person or group whose interests can be best served at the expense of another person or group. Some teachers exploit their students for emotional reasons, as do some husbands or wives their spouses or parents their children. Many city governments, at least in America, exploit the taxpayers who have little redress against the misuse of their money through corruption and nepotism in high places. Whenever we take advantage of someone's need and so employ him cheaply we are exploiting him, although it may look like charity. Our own era also abounds in remote, impersonal and even in some respects apparently benign forms of exploitation. The faceless bureaucracies organizing welfare services; the vast corporations whose intricate filaments enter unrecognized into every aspect of our existence helping us to meet the needs they have themselves stimulated; the educational systems in which we eagerly place our children and where they learn competitive materialism and the skills with which to serve the exploitative network – all these things use us and, in using us, increase. Often we are completely unaware of how we are being used and it is a vitally important part of our education for liberation – from these forces among other things – to learn to recognize them. Any curriculum for social change should help us to do so.

Often the position of the exploited looks hopeless. The idea of moral or political power sufficient to oppose the material force with which vested interest protects itself may seem a dream. But they have one trump card. *In the last resort the oppressors are powerless without the oppressed.* They depend upon the oppressed for labour, for support, for investments, and for the sense of their own righteousness. It is the recognition of this aspect of their power which will enable the weak to become strong enough to challenge and change the exploitative networks on both large scale and small.

C. CHANGING SOCIETY

The part of the curriculum concerned with this subtopic would draw heavily on case studies. These could include the integration movement in the southern states in the late 1950s and early 1960s, the work of Danilo Dolci in fighting the Mafia in Sicily, the little-known but extraordinary non-violent insurrection in El Salvador in 1944 (Lakey and Parkman, 1969), the strike of Russian political prisoners at Vorkuta camp in 1953 (Scholmer, 1955), the French student rising of 1968 which, despite violent episodes, practically brought down the French government by largely non-violent means (Cohn-Bendit, 1968), the California grape strike organized by Caesar Chavez (Matthiessen, 1969), non-violent resistance in Czechoslovakia after the Russian invasion in 1968 (Remington, 1970), passive resistance in South Africa (Kuper, 1957), the struggle of the Quakers to live and worship in Massachusetts Bay Colony between 1656 and 1675 (Lakey, undated), the remarkably effective non-violent resistance against the Nazis in occupied Europe, especially in Norway, Denmark, and the Netherlands during World War II (Roberts, 1969), and of course the Indian Independence movement led by Mahatma Gandhi.[7]

---

[7] Apart from works already mentioned, the reader is referred to the excellent bibliography, comprehensive but manageable, in Sharp (1970), pp. 146–9.

The study of these and other cases is both illuminating and encouraging. The Norwegians, Danes and Dutch had, of course, an unfortunately long period to perfect a technique of resistance against the occupying Nazi forces which, German generals told Liddell Hart (1969), they found more unnerving and hard to combat than armed resistance; that they understood and knew how to deal with on their own terms. Strikes, demonstrations, sabotage, rejection of all social overtures, complete non-co-operation, the constant flouting of regulations, and the maintenance of strong morale by underground news media thoroughly confused and worried the Germans, tying up numbers of troops and distracting them from the developing dangers of the second front. The Czechs had, in 1968, much less time to organize themselves against the domination of the Russians. Nevertheless they acted with an extraordinarily effective spontaneity which not only largely prevented Russian violence, but greatly reduced collaboration. The Czechs believe that had they used violent methods instead of strikes, counter-propaganda, passive resistance and persuasion, they would have lost even more than they did as well as suffering innumerable casualties as compared with a very small number who were actually killed. In these examples, the Russians and the Nazis were impeded but not defeated. In El Salvador, however, a non-violent resistance movement initiated by students and joined subsequently by bus and taxi drivers, then by shop-keepers, doctors, bankers and clergy, led to the ousting of a dictator, amnesty for offenders and general elections. Here again, the weapons were strikes, non-co-operation, demonstrations and the wearing of mourning. The much better known French student uprising was within an ace of achieving equal success; ultimately, of course, widespread violence broke out and the ill-armed students were defeated. But the real effectiveness of the movement lay in its non-violent dislocation of almost all services. Non-violent resistance in the American South during the 1960s and in South Africa followed more the Gandhian principles than those of civilian resistance to an invader; there was a greater admixture of persuasion in the defiance. It should be pointed out, however, that persuasion (or conversion, see below) was not completely absent even in such desperate circumstances as those facing the Czechs. There are many reports that the potential violence of Russian soldiers was neutralized by Czechs who approached and earnestly asked if they could really bring themselves to shoot civilians. Of course the most successful, and most publicized, campaign of non-violent social change was that waged in India chiefly under the inspiration of Gandhi. It is interesting to note, however, that many of the methods and principles which are known as Gandhian are by no means new. Some of them were employed three hundred years ago by the persecuted Quakers in the Massachusetts Bay Colony whose courage and calm defiance of the fanatical persecution practised upon them, eventually won the freedom they demanded. Dolci and Chavez, who have successfully attacked economic and social exploitation, currently exemplify the resourcefulness, courage, toughness and organizational ability which alone enable the weak to defy the strong, and not only to confront them but to extract concessions and even to defeat them. What this means, of course, is that the weak have in effect become the strong; power is the capacity to create uncertainty and power is a function of determination, ingenuity, organization, and moral strength as much as it is of arms and armies. It was these qualities that enabled the prisoners at Vorkuta in their desperation to achieve so many of their limited objectives – not freedom, but tolerable conditions in their servitude.

In addition to studying these and comparable examples, teachers and students should all identify and examine ways in which people have been led or compelled, without violence, to make or agree to changes which are not to their advantage, or which they had initially resisted even if later their disinclination to change was overcome. These should not all be taken from the more dramatic political scene. We should examine the situation in which a selfish child agrees to share his plaything, or a house-proud mother her house, in which a teacher abandons an authoritarian disciplinary technique, or a school committee gives up some of its power.

The study of these cases, besides being interesting and encouraging, should enable students to grasp and elaborate general principles. If this can be done, non-violent action for social change will seem easier, less dependent on inspiration than on common sense. Courage, nerve and persistence it will always require, but if we know the rules of the game we will be able to make those cool evaluations without which bravery becomes foolhardiness and persistence becomes unintelligent stubbornness.

Others much more learned and experienced than myself will elaborate the theoretical framework of the curriculum. What follows is the most tentative outline of a possible system for teaching the theory of non-violent action.

The most important element in achieving social change is the level of awareness of those who would make the change. There are innumerable instances of oppressed situations which could have been changed overnight if all the oppressed groups had defied their oppressors. I have in mind particularly South Africa. There was a period around 1961, before the present regime was as firmly entrenched as it is today, when many well-informed persons were persuaded that a massive programme of non-co-operation and boycotting by the black population could compel the government to make major changes. This may or may not have been true. The salient fact is, however, that the black population was not ready to take part in such a programme. Only 1 per cent belonged to the revolutionary (and non-violent) African National Congress, and attempts to organize a national strike of Africans failed miserably because of the low general level of awareness. In this context awareness meant, obviously, more than consciousness that the government's policies – to put it very mildly – favoured the whites more than the blacks. Virtually everyone knew that, but over the generations (though things had been getting a little better in some respects under the previous government) they had come to expect it. It was inevitable, that is how the world was and the only thing to do was to make the best of a bad situation. Awareness implies a degree of understanding of the situation, recognition of the de-humanizing being done, hope that the right action can change the situation.

The first task of the revolutionary leader, then, is to carry out a form of education. His people must be brought to understand what their circumstances are doing to them and to realize that they are not entirely without power to change them; indeed, that if enough people reach this awareness strongly enough they have irresistible power. This education is carried out in a number of dimensions, by words, including the development of a new vocabulary of liberation that Paulo Freire (1970) calls renaming the world, by examples of defiance which demonstrate that the apparently omnipotent authority *can* be defied, and by affectionate understanding of the fear and ignorance which would hold many back from action. Education is also the continuing and the last task. In this connection I should draw particular attention to the work of Freire just mentioned. He is, so far as I know, the only contemporary educational expert who has devised a technique of education for liberation. His work with illiterates in Brazil convinced him that education frequently served as a technique of oppression. Students learned a vocabulary which – with its middle-class words denoting middle-class affluence and social values – emphasized their own poverty, differentness and failure, giving them a sense of futility and inferiority. But learning to read and write is, Freire stresses, an act of knowing. The choice of what Freire terms generative words, those which have social and personal significance, can lead to a perception of the self and society which he calls consciencization and I call awareness. Freire's methods of teaching literacy through building on these key words until the student's awareness has expanded to fill the former illiterates' environment and to give him impetus to change it, is remarkably affective.

There are no limits to the awareness needed by the revolutionary movement; particularly at the stage when it assumes power, it must be conscious of the peril of being trapped by it, of becoming itself oppressive. I would add, finally, that it is not only the leaders who educate the masses but the masses who educate themselves. William Hinton, in his extraordinary book, *Fanshen*

94

(1966), which means turning over or transformation, gives the case history of a Chinese village which educates itself. Given the seminal idea, the initial quantum of awareness, the people constructed for themselves a new consciousness which strengthened them to oppose the inertia of tradition and selfishness in themselves and would undoubtedly have strengthened them to oppose an external enemy. Education, then, is the preliminary, the concomitant and the sequel to efforts to achieve social change.

These efforts, if successful, lead either to change by conversion or change by coercion. Sharp (1970), recognizes another form of change which he terms accommodation. This tends to occur in a situation in which the opponent has not exactly been converted, in that he does not believe in the changes that take place, nor has he been coerced, in that he has not been forced to make them. On the other hand, he now sees that the issue is not particularly important, that the activists are not particularly bad people. Consequently, in order to avoid what he now sees as unnecessary trouble, he gives in with good grace. Although I recognize this category of change, I believe that it is normally brought about by the sorts of action leading to conversion or coercion, or both. For this reason I do not consider it separately.

To convert one's opponent is to make his awareness extend to oneself, one's people and their plight. This is likely to be difficult. Although one is often delightfully surprised to find sympathy and interest in unexpected places, those who control a situation we wish to change (but not necessarily others who are in their camp because of the accident of birth rather than conviction) are likely to see us as a threat. We menace their belonging-identity, their property and position. In consequence they fear and hate us, justifying these negative emotions with falsifications about our wickedness and immorality. The more active we are the more will we be detested. It is only possible to break through the wall of antipathy and incomprehension by administering shocks to the sensibility of our opponents.

The first and fundamental shock is to treat them absolutely differently from the way in which they treat us. To smile when they frown, to speak gently when they rant, to treat them with dignity when they insult us, to avoid humiliating them when they deride us, to behave towards them as human beings when they treat us as animals. This is the importance of the first part of the curriculum. It must become deeply part of us, because we could not otherwise act with conviction. Our smiles would be false, our politeness a mockery, our hearts full of hatred. We would become then an even easier prey for our oppressors. If, however, we can school our awareness to accept these enemies as human beings, to feel for them in the confusion and anxiety we are causing them, to reach out to them for a common solution to our common problem, the shell of self-interest surrounding their awareness may be cracked.

Yet again, if we are steadfast and friendly in the suffering and privation they may inflict upon us, their perception of us and our cause may change. This is all the more likely if we and our opponents come from approximately the same social situation. If they can see us bearing our punishment or discomfort in cheerful fortitude, they are more apt to give us their attention than if we are different from them – by religion, colour, language, nationality, etc. – so that they can dismiss our strange behaviour as the aberration of our group.

Perhaps the keynote of our attempt to convert our enemy is the deeply held belief that he, no less than ourselves, needs liberation. If our dignity is impugned by being oppressed, so is his by oppressing. We are part of the same system and the humanity of both is diminished. We, in fact, have the advantage because we know what is happening. He only has the material rewards, so often hollow, of the oppressor's system – how affluent, for example, is the average Southern white?

We do not convert, of course, merely through passivity. We do not simply smile with Christian forgiveness as we are hustled off to jail. On the contrary, we do something forceful and potent which makes us a threat worthy of imprisonment – and this, of course, is often the tactic of coercion which will be discussed shortly.

We speak and write and try to convince people that inequality and injustice and corruption are wrong and destroy those who practise them as much as, and indeed more than, those who suffered them. But above all we have to *feel* and to *be*, to a point where our message cannot be ignored. Of course this may take time. As Gandhi wrote, 'every good movement passes through five stages: indifference, ridicule, abuse, repression and respect.' He urged restraint at the critical moment when eventually abuse changed to repression, because either to be cowed or to retaliate with violence would spoil everything and waste the long period of preparation and slow growth of awareness. 'Violence is suicide,' he said (Bose, p. 264).

To induce change through coercion is to mobilize the latent power of the oppressed. This is the power, no less, to bring the system to a standstill, to jeopardize all those vested interests which the rulers wish to preserve by not changing the system. The danger here is that they recognize the nature of the threat more clearly than those who impose it, make concessions which satisfy the less sophisticated rebels, but leave the basic structure intact. If, however, the activists are sufficiently astute, they can achieve a position of great strength. If their organization has been adequate and the preparatory educational work intensive and widespread, they can gain mastery.

Their weapons here are somewhat different from those aimed at conversion – demonstrations, entering restaurants or transport forbidden to a particular group, panning salt – the Indian revolutionaries' harmless contravention of an absurd regulation– and so on. These are actions of defiance aiming not only to awaken the conscience of the oppressors, but also to educate (in the revolutionary sense in which I use the word in this chapter) the masses of the oppressed whose awareness is low. The weapons for coercion, on the other hand, consist of strikes, boycotts, working to rule, massive civil disobedience, planned confusion and muddle, the dislocation of communications, innumerable acts of quiet unidentifiable sabotage, the commission of offences on such a scale as to virtually immobilize the police and swamp the jails, above all and in every way the refusal to serve the oppressive regime and to damage its efficiency by all possible expedients.

Such a campaign would no doubt have its casualties. In brutal and oppressive regimes they might be heavy. On the other hand, they would be very much smaller than if a virtually unarmed population took the violent route and spitted itself upon the sophisticated weaponry of an oppressor group – as would undoubtedly happen if, for example, the black South Africans were to rise in angry desperation against the whites.

In order to wage this type of struggle it is essential to involve great numbers – hence the necessity for education, and to have developed a highly efficient organization. (A part of the curriculum might well be devoted to organization building under difficult conditions.) It is also essential to have clearly analysed the oppressive system in order to know how best to immobilize it and to bring it to its knees. (Here another part of the curriculum could well discuss ways of identifying the nodal points of various types of organization and system.)

It would be stressed, however, that this tough, difficult and dangerous opposition to the physically strong by the physically weak is not incompatible with conversion. It is perfectly possible to oppose without hating. It is possible to destroy the oppressor's system of exploitation while feeling compassion for his perplexity and despair and seeking ways of integrating him into the more equitable order which, it is hoped, will emerge. It should be noted in this connection that aristocrats became convinced communists in Russia and landlords experienced fanshen in China.

D. CONVENTIONAL TECHNIQUES OF SOCIAL CHANGE

I have left to the last the more conventional, or constitutional techniques of achieving social change through political activity, legal reform, civil liberties associations and the like which operate within the law though often against many dominant trends of society. The study of these should not be neglected, for it is through such means that many revolutionary reforms have been brought about – for example, in the character of English rural life, and through the legitimate operations of labour unions despite the prostitution to which, from time to time, they have been subject. To work through these techniques may be difficult. It may evoke hostility from those whose interests are clearly being threatened, and many left-wing politicians whose activities are completely legal have suffered extreme unpopularity.

It should be made clear, however, that those who employ the lawful and legitimate techniques of social change may be fighting stronger opponents with their own weapons: this was not the case in what we considered in the last section. If they do so, they will lose unless they have so awakened popular awareness and so planned their strategy that their force is irresistible.

We must also face the danger that our efforts will be swamped, obfuscated and turned around by a more powerful opponent. We may be bought off by minor concessions, or made to seem nagging critics, traitors at worst, of a regime which may not be perfect but is doing its best to serve the people of the country. In short our attempts to apply legitimate techniques may simply mean that we lose the game, and perhaps our own souls to boot, to a stronger and more ruthless opponent who occupies a position in the system enabling him to hold the trump cards.

I frequently remember that it was actually President Eisenhower, a moderately conservative military man and a decent human being, who warned America and the world against the encroaching power of the military-industrial complex. If such a man perceived the danger, how great it must have been. Now, after more than a decade, how much greater it must have become, and not only in the United States. In a sense it epitomizes the system and has a large measure of control over its administrative and political mechanisms. We must consider seriously whether this situation can be brought under human control by the conventional constitutional means.

E. PRACTICE

Studies in these preceding four sections of the curriculum should, wherever possible, be applied. Students should be provided with first-hand experience of techniques of social change. When an actual setting is not available (and clearly this could not be pre-arranged), debates, simulations, encounter group experience, meetings with people of other religious, social or racial groups for discussion of differences or common problems, should be organized. In planning practical work it should be borne in mind that, apart from major political issues such as, recently, the Vietnam war, there are always many smaller local issues. These may involve employment practices, municipal corruption, discrimination of various sorts, apparent miscarriages of justice, victimization at school or work and so on. These should be studied and, where appropriate, acted upon.

8

Two Educational Institutions

My ideal school can only have come into existence when the transformations considered in the last chapter have occurred, when we are no longer controlled by the old system or are impelled by material and psychological pressures to educate our young to its service. Until then we have to act in a piecemeal fashion, subverting the system and its techniques of indoctrination through schooling as best we can by our own teaching methods and, in suitable circumstances, curricula for social change.

However, if I had the resources and/or the organizational ability, I could set up an educational institution (school is not an appropriate word) serving as a preliminary model for the school of the future. It would be like this:

Children would come at nursery or kindergarten age and from then through the next seven or eight years the education would be based on what is termed the English 'free school'.[8] Education at this stage carried out in this way is not a commodity; it is as unrelated to the system as is possible anywhere within the system and combines (or should combine) – as in the Cambridge Friends School (attended as I write by my daughter Deborah, amongst others) – the best of affective education, with the type of

[8] The best analysis of these is perhaps contained in the Plowden Report; Central Advisory Council for Education (England) (1971). American readers will find the most accessible comprehensive account of new trends in English primary education in Silberman (1970) Chapter 6, pp. 208–64.

relationship between teachers and students which I have tried to describe.

The teachers would be selected for a combination of professional craftsmanship and wisdom (or awareness); the two may not be unrelated. They would not only serve as teachers of particular subjects or groups, but, at least some of them, as advisers to students at any stage of their passage through the institution. It would be their task, so far as possible, to be concerned with the development of awareness as opposed to the academic progress of their students. (The level of awareness would no doubt, however, influence aspects of academic progress.) They would be concerned with the growth of the whole person, with helping students to have the experiences and to gain the knowledge enabling them to mature in vision, judgement and sensitivity. They would be less like the conventional concept of a teacher than the ideal tutor of a bygone age, a spiritual confessor, or a guru.

The major differences would begin to appear at approximately the stage where secondary education starts in most parts of the world. In one sense a key aspect of difference would be the continuation into higher grades of what prevailed at lower ones, but with a widening sweep of subjects studied at great depth. Literature, history, mathematics and biology, for example, would be explored with greater freedom because there would be no set periods or formal requirements. The curriculum on social change, begun at an elementary level by emphasizing mutual respect and care, could be studied in its full range, with historical, sociological and economic corollaries developed in parallel studies.

This work would not, however, normally be directed towards gaining entry into higher education or professions. The grades would not be given, nor the tests taken which would ensure the routine progression into the system. If, however, any student were worried or dissatisfied and wished to proceed in a more traditional way, he would be awarded the grades, etc., which would enable him to transfer into another institution of a more conventional type.

Our institution would, in effect, be helping to give birth to a new sort of human being. I say helping because there are already many of them around. Many of the more aware young men and women are completely dissatisfied with formal education as it exists on a virtually world-wide basis (perhaps not in China, Tanzania and a few other places). They see it as being largely meaningless except as a means of entering a system which they consider evil. So they go through it without enthusiasm for the process (often despite interest in particular topics or teachers), or they drop out. Those who stay in, pass into the professional job market to do work they largely scorn but for which they see no alternative. Others drift around, often unsatisfied intellectually and working, if at all, at unrewarding and trivial tasks.

Our institution would attempt to make explicit the frequently confused reservations which these young people have about society and work. It would aim to give them an education in both awareness and intellectual fields which could assist them to relate their own lives to the world, neither by joining the system nor by floating precariously on the fringe, but by doing work which gave real satisfaction, either because it was of service or because it stretched mind, imagination and dexterity – or in fact did both.

At any stage after, say, the early teens, students who so wished would be helped to learn a craft or skill, working at it part time or full time. Very often this would mean leaving the institution, for the skill would require ateliers, workshops, garages, or agencies which no educational institution could hope to comprise. In other instances the school would be able to arrange more directly for the appropriate learning experience within or without its walls. Special sorts of relationships – types of apprenticeships – would be worked out with individuals; groups of students with similar concerns would study together; the resources of libraries and computer-stored information would be tapped. Ivan Illich (1971, pp. 72–104) has made a delightfully imaginative list of such devices. But in either case the understanding, or at any rate the hope would be for their return to the institution to integrate their skill or trade with their awareness and with their intellectual understanding of society, of their work, and of their role in life. Indeed their return to the institution for a type of regenerative retreat, if only for a few days, should occur periodically throughout life, especially after major changes of estate.

During these periods and indeed throughout the whole educational experience, use would be made of mental techniques which are seldom seen as part of normal education. These are pondering and meditation. To ponder in this context is to allow the mind to play with imaginative reflection around a topic. I recall hearing of a great French biologist who gave a fish to his student, telling him to discover what he could about it. The young man returned after an hour having identified its species, weighed and measured it, photographed it and discovered its sex. But he was told he had only begun to learn about the fish; he was to think more about it and return later. Several hours afterwards, having dissected it and subjected it to a variety of tests, he came back only to be told again to go away and think. This time he stayed away several days, pondering deeply upon the facts he had discovered, recognizing relationships, seeing inferences and implications, understanding things about fish in particular, aquatic life in general, and living things as a whole. This time the teacher was satisfied. The young people in our institution would be encouraged to ponder and helped to develop this little understood mental art which is, nevertheless, accessible to all and appropriate to all ages. Meditation, as I use the word, is less if an intellectual process than pondering. It is more an emptying of the mind of those things which plague it and distract it from the process of thinking. It provides a respite from the ennervating action of negative emotion and is an essential preliminary and accompaniment to all creative activity, including pondering. I was interested that in Herman Hesse's extraordinary imaginative *tour de force The Glass Bead Game* (1943, 1969 edition), the dedicated and austere but completely secular Castalian intellectuals regularly practised oriental and other forms of meditation. Hesse recognized how vital this is to the controlled health of the mind. There are, of course, systems of meditation, good and bad, extremely hard and relatively easy, in abundance. I would not prescribe any particular method. I would point out, however, that many Quaker schools have regular Meetings for silent worship which are not only appreciated by those having religious beliefs. The smallest children, in fact, can understand the meaning of inner quiet and feel the value of a peaceful and undistracted mind.

The current structure of professional life would, of course, preclude entry into medicine, law, engineering and most other jobs having authority, prestige and high salaries. Access to the arts, skilled crafts and of course a wide range of manual work would be much easier. But there are some fields which, though in general requiring degrees or similar qualifications, would not be impossibly exclusive. There is an interestingly wide range of social service activities; of less formal teaching in free, store-front or street-corner schools; there are possibilities of employment as research assistants in laboratories or to scholars in various fields; there are libraries which require intelligent work demanding initiative but not formal qualifications.

The mission of the students of our institution would not only be to make satisfying and valuable lives for themselves, but to demonstrate that they can make important contributions without having the normal qualifications, perhaps for the very reason that they have not laboured for the qualifications and in the process had the imagination and independence knocked out of them.

One might object that if they are going to work, particularly in a semi-professional capacity, at a formal job, they should be allowed the qualification – even if the training is of little value – which would give them a position commensurate with their ability. There are several answers. In the first place, jobs are seldom commensurate with ability; they depend upon the type of diploma or degree, 'intelligence' tests, the college record, the level of literacy of their referees, and above all, their capacity to perform in a way which pleases the system. Then again, if knowledge is used to buy into the system, it is all the more easy for us to become committed to a particular life style and so, of course, to be tied ever more firmly to our profession. It would be axiomatic in our institution that commitment to a particular job was not final. It was simply what seemed appropriate at one stage in the individual's life. As our lives move forward, and if we lead them properly, we change; and these changes should be reflected in our habits of life and especially our work. I know that I have changed greatly during the twenty-five years of my professional life and have played different roles, although most of the time I have had a university base. I have served as an adviser on development to foreign governments, have acted as a mediator in political disputes, and have radically shifted the focus of my intellectual interests five or six times. One might say I am fortunate to have been able to do all this without changing my basic academic identity, but I might have been forced to more radical honesty and greater effectiveness if my shifts of pace and emphasis had required more sacrifice. In addition I should reaffirm that acceptance of this way of life I am describing would be entirely voluntary. Those who adopted it would do so because its flexibility and relative independence of the system suited them. Also because they wished to demonstrate that competence and qualification need not necessarily coincide.

I should emphasize finally that it is not to professional education as such that I object, but the implication that the training (or, more properly, the qualification) secures a place in the hierarchy. But the extent to which we are captured by the stratified society is a function of our level of awareness. This form of education has as its prime concern the raising of awareness, and those whose awareness is sufficiently high could enter the formal professions without succumbing to the attractions of competitive materialism. Indeed, if the unpeaceful society is to be successfully opposed, it would be vital that there be awakened individuals in its every professional arena – in the law, in the churches, in business, in medicine, in science and technology, and of course in education. Therefore, if the students of my imagined institution conceived that they could best fulfil their role in changing society as lawyers, doctors, physicists, ministers, or business executives, ways should be found of helping them to prepare for these roles and of assisting them in moving to more specialized training.

These young people, then, would be purposeful. Indeed to a large extent the object of their education would be to endow them with purpose. They would not be drifters, though they might modulate, but this would be appropriate to each stage of their development, from job to job, interest to interest, and not because of boredom, inertia or aimlessness; and some might just as easily select a lasting interest to begin with. They would be literate and well-balanced. Above all, they would seek to bring about the peaceful society. It is hard to predict the future of such a venture. An important underlying aim would be to create an understanding, respect, and finally a need for this approach to the process and purpose of education. Much, of course, would depend upon the products themselves. However, even if they constantly demonstrated their valuable qualities, the implications of this form of education might be rejected. For one thing, it makes a frontal assault on too many educational and professional vested interests, and a less-direct attack upon the basic fabric of the system vital to those interests. It would therefore be feared and rejected by many. For another thing, quite apart from the hostility they may arouse, it is simply very hard to gain acceptance for a new class or type of people. In the mid-1950s I was to some extent involved in the attempt to establish social work as a professional activity in Pakistan. With United Nations assistance, a department of social welfare had been set up in the university of the Panjab in Lahore and a master's degree was granted to those who passed the course. My task was to make plans for their employment in various fields where they were desperately needed. But the Ministry of Finance would not sanction the allocation of money until the appropriate department had created the posts, while the department would not create the posts until the cash was available. This impasse lasted for months, and many of the newly-trained graduates in social work returned in disgust to their old jobs, but not all. Eventually the pressure of this new professional group forced the bureaucrats out of their fixed positions and the much-needed work began to be done. The analogy is not, of course, close. Things were far easier in Pakistan than they would be in the case we are now considering. But even there more than official stubbornness was involved. Up until that time social work had largely been the prerogative of society ladies, the wives of the official caste who were making the difficulties and many (not, to their honour, all) did not want the fashionable glamour of orphans' bazaars and formal openings of homes for fallen women to be replaced by the toughly prosaic common sense of professional workers. But the lesson is that changes take place because people, through their quality and purposefulness, force themselves upon the attention. If they were able to do so, these young people might represent an increasingly acceptable model for the future.

Since I am indulging in fantasy, or perhaps I should say futurology, I might as well go the whole way and speculate about what these ideas might mean if, inconceivably, I had a free hand in reshaping the institution in which I recently worked, the Harvard Graduate School of Education (H.G.S.E.).[9] I hasten to say that what follows is in no sense a reflection on our excellent deans Ted Sizer and Paul Yevisaker, for whose educational wisdom and personal stature I have the warmest admiration. Few men could have done more for the School and I am convinced that I would have not been able to thread the Harvard mazes, to reconcile a dozen conflicting interests, to preserve my sanity and sense of humour, to follow consistently my academic conscience and to come up with a structure half as valuable as they have done. But when one writes about what one would like to do, one is not subject to the awesome constraints affecting the academic administrator in real life; consequently I am giving my imagination free rein.

[9] Those who are interested in an earlier concept of the nature and function of the H.G.S.E. should consult *The Graduate Study of Education* (The Sheffler Report) (1965). A subsequent unpublished report – Curle and Whitten (1968) – takes a stand which is perhaps between the views of the Scheffler Report and those expressed in the book, but nearer the latter.

When I began to discuss some of the ideas in this book with groups of students in my seminar, they would naturally compare the principles and practices we had been talking about with those prevalent in the H.G.S.E. These discussions were sometimes to the detriment of the former, sometimes of the latter. When asked my opinion, I would usually try to reconcile the two, pointing out that the School was large and diverse, a university in miniature, which inevitably and properly contained many contradictory parts and principles. One could find, if one sought them, elements which corresponded to what our seminar in general favoured and others which did not. I still believe this, but my ideas have to some extent clarified and I am able now to take a rather more definite line.

The School, as it was constituted in 1971 after a series of searching discussions, comprised six main areas, as they are called. These deal with (1) Administration, Social and Educational Policy, and Planning which includes three so-called shops dealing with these separate overlapping fields (my personal place was in the third); (2) Human Development, which speaks for itself, though it should be explained that it is principally concerned with adolescents; (3) a small group studying the Philosophy of Education; (4) Education in Early Childhood; (5) Clinical Psychology and Public Practice, a programme run jointly with two other faculties; (6) Learning Environments, involving the study of relationships between learning and the total context in which it is carried out.

The students within these programmes, with one exception to be noted, are engaged in the long drawn-out struggle to obtain doctorates. For the most part they may expect to be appointed to specialized positions within the education or psychological professions. They will become school administrators, at various levels, teachers of educational psychology, teachers of philosophy, researchers in human development, planners, policy makers and the like. The programmes in learning environments and early childhood education may, when their character has stabilized (they have only been recently initiated) produce more practitioners, but in general people with doctorates do not teach: they tell others how to set about the job they are not themselves doing – this at any rate has often been true of myself.

There are two other programmes at the lower level of the masters degree. The first is the Masters of Arts in Teaching (M.A.T.) which is the equivalent of the English Graduate Diploma in Education. The second is the Masters in Education for General Purposes (M.Ed.). The detailed programme of the former depends to a considerable extent on the subjects which the student will teach and includes practice teaching under supervision. The latter is an extraordinarily flexible course, with virtually no formal requirements beyond the completion of eight half courses in an academic year of two semesters. Most of the students, provided they have a helpful adviser, pick an appropriate and stimulating combination of courses. Their interests vary greatly and many of them are the more experienced people to whom I have previously referred. They have all sorts of different reasons for applying to join this programme, and taking the combination of courses they select. It is to be hoped that many return enriched to their previous work, or branch out fruitfully into something new. Some, the exceptions I referred to earlier, are really interested in one or another of the doctoral programmes, become unofficially attached to them and, with luck, get fully admitted to them in the following year. For the rest, however, the M.Ed. programme is or should be, if they use it well, a fascinating year of intellectual reconnaissance. This is its strength. Its weakness is that for most people, except the embyro specialists, it can be no more than reconnaissance; there is little chance to develop closer and deeper acquaintance with any one of the subjects sampled. A further weakness is that it is a programme in education, rather than teaching and may not be much use in helping many people carry out what is, after all, the central function of education.

Here I should point to an ancient controversy about the H.G.S.E. According to same, the School, which although large by English standards is small by American ones, should concentrate on training educational leaders, the highly qualified administrators and specialists in more academic disciplines who will exert national influence; it should not try to compete with the great mass producers of teachers, for after all the average young teacher is not going to have much impact on the profession.[10] The other point of view is that education is about teaching and that we should therefore not neglect to train teachers; indeed we should set an example of teacher quality, if not match the quality of other institutions. On the whole, the first argument has tended to prevail.

My proposal for the H.G.S.E. is as follows:

We should keep the existing general arrangement, perhaps with some modifications, but these would undoubtedly be made in any case and I need not attempt to suggest them. The difference would be in the overall orientation of the doctoral programmes. They should be thought of primarily as intellectual powerhouses for an entirely new programme in teaching which would replace both M.A.T. and M.Ed. Students within these specialized programmes would be research scholars, a fact which would be emphasized by awarding them (if the University would agree) the degree of Ph.D. instead of Ed.D.

The teaching programme would last three or four years. It would be general in character, as is the training which leads to a degree in law or medicine. My personal preference would be that no degree were awarded at its completion, merely the statement that so and so had successfully carried out a course in teacher education and practical teaching. However, I recognize that if students attend a university which, unlike the institution I have just described, does award degrees, it is rather too much to expect that they should forgo the prize. This should, if anything, be the degree of Doctor of Education, doctor because of the length and intensity of the training, education to emphasize the professional character of the qualification.

The prime quality to be sought in the candidates would, as in my fantasy of the future, be their high level of awareness,

[10] This is in essence the point of view of *The Graduate Study of Education* (1965).

their maturity and the richness of their experience. The high calibre of present applicants shows that there would be no shortage of such suitably qualified people. Academic qualifications would be of secondary importance; there would be time, perhaps during the fourth year, for refurbishing subject matter.

Training would cover four main areas:

1. *Children:* Their behaviour; their development – intellectual physical and moral; adolescence; problems of early childhood; and so on.

2. *Society as a setting within which education occurs:* urban problems; social change; the interrelations of education and society; exploitation, oppression and deprivation and their effects on and relation to education; race and class; problems of administering education.

3. *The theory and practice of teaching:* the learning relationship; relationships between children in the educational setting; conditions which stultify and those which stimulate; affective education; the value and limitations of sensitivity training; and above all practice teaching in a diversity of settings throughout the programme.

4. *Subjects to be taught.*

I am not so egocentric as to suppose that such a programme would necessarily be influenced by the sorts of ideas I have expressed in this book, nor that it would have no value if it did not. I simply believe that an arrangement of this sort would produce persons having great value to education. They would, amongst other things, be well suited to teach in my imagined institution and would be the forerunners of the elected teachers of the future. Such a programme is not, I think, impractical. The resources required to run it already exist in the H.G.S.E. There would be no marked change in emphasis from scholarly academic to general work of a practical character; there are in fact already practitioners and the intellectual stimulus to be derived from the researchers would be as important as ever. The difficulty I envisage is rather one of co-ordinating independent scholars in highly autonomous shops to ensure that they provided a proper and balanced range of course offerings for the training programme.

Graduates of this teaching programme would be at liberty later to register, with some concessions for the work they had already done, for one of the specialized programmes. There should, however, be an interval filled with several years of practical experience between taking the two programmes.

POSTSCRIPT

As I have noted, the description of the H.G.S.E. dates back to 1971 when this book was drafted. Since then some things have changed and I considered rewriting my account of the School, but for two reasons decided not to. Firstly, the principles I have tried to outline remain unaltered; secondly, those who know the institution may be interested in considering whether things have (or have not) moved in the direction I advocate.

9

A Special Case: Education and Development in Poor Countries

Most of my work during the last seventeen or eighteen years has been concerned with problems of development in the poor nations, and particularly of the role of education therein. Having written three books and countless shorter pieces on this topic, I have now reached the point where I believe that most of what I wrote was wrong. I assumed firstly that a desirable condition which I (and most other people) termed development could be achieved in very large part through economic growth. Secondly, that economic growth would be attained through appropriately adapting the practices of the rich nations, and especially through the aid which these nations could supply. Thirdly, I saw education, or human resource development as we termed it, as a powerful tool in the achievement of economic development; it provided the people with the skills upon which development depends; it spread opportunity, having a levelling and equalizing effect on society and creating a new class of persons owing their position to education and ability rather than birth; it created a leaven of hope.

I now reject my first assumption because the model has lost its attraction. The 'developed' countries are destroying the biosphere with their wastes, their callous rapacity is using up the world's resources at awful speed, they are inextricably enmeshed in interminable conflicts, they are plagued internally by crime and violence, tensions between the races and the generations are growing increasingly dangerous and damaging, they abound in every sort of unpeacefulness. Above all it is clear that they make ruthless use of those less powerful than themselves. This leads to the failure of my second assumption: the rich countries as a whole exploit the poor countries and in fact are impeding rather than promoting their economic advance. The rich countries buy the raw materials of the poor countries cheaply and sell them back manufactured goods at high cost. Even when they set up industries in the poor countries, with the ostensible advantage making cheaper products available, the poor country's economy suffers. Because foreign corporations import from the parent companies they discriminate against local suppliers; they swamp local initiative and overwhelm less up-to-date local industry; they keep control of managerial positions and the technology in their own hands; they produce nothing for export if export would conflict with other branches of the corporations.

The bulk of the aid which is given to the poor countries is either military assistance which binds them to the politico-strategic camp of the donor or is of economic advantage to him. To be sure, some aid has no direct economic, political or strategic strings attached and appears to be purely altruistic. Indeed much good work has been done in agriculture, social welfare, community development, aspects of education and the like. These constitute the sugar coating. The total effect of the loans, investments and technical assistance given by the rich to the poor has, however, been to enrich those who gave it, either directly or by creating new demands and markets for their goods. Even when assistance is dispensed by international agencies, the World Bank or the International Monetary Fund (but not the United Nations which is too representative), it has these effects and is suspected by poor nations which prize their independence. I am not accusing these agencies of exploitative intent, but the fact is that they are dominated by the rich nations and the rich nations are dominated by the idea that development – and indeed happiness – depend upon consumption. To act on this belief inevitably leads to the imposition of rich country standards upon the poor, which ends by enslaving them.

The recipients of aid, on the whole, have either benefited less than the donors or in many cases have actually been depleted by it. As I observed in the first few pages of this book, global poverty and hunger are now worse than they were twenty years ago when international aid was getting into its stride. There is, however, an important exception to this general tendency. As the representatives of the rich nations in the poor countries increased in numbers, as the colonial officials were replaced with technical experts, foreign advisers, representatives of a host of agencies and above all by business men, so a new national *élite* began to emerge. These were the local agents of the foreign corporations, officials who smoothed the way, ministers and others whose good will it was desirable to purchase, labour leaders who could control the workers. It is this group that has really profited from aid and foreign investment. The local contracts, the gifts, the high salaries, the privileges, the opportunities for travel and scholarships abroad, the chances of investment, have created a considerable class of persons throughout most of the Third World who depend on and profit from the link with the rich nations and who are, in turn, essential to them. These people with their wealthy masters, constitute the exploitative network. Together they spoliate the poor countries. It is ironical that the same conditions obtain between the rich countries and the poor countries, as between the rich sectors of the poor countries, where the international interests are concentrated, and the poor, mainly rural, hinterlands. The wealth flows from poor to rich, and the rich are ever more able to impose impoverishing demands upon the poor. But even the affluence of the poor country *élites* (or to be fair, sections of them) cannot save in exceptional cases do much to increase national wealth, however unevenly distributed.[11]

The failure of my third assumption is the most disappointing because it was the most idealistic. Education has indeed spread widely and has been felt by many to be the symbol of emancipation. As it has spread, so hope has burgeoned. But the education that has spread was essentially the education of the rich

[11] In so brief an exposition of complex arguments a great deal must be left undocumented. Anyone who wishes to pursue the point of view put forward in this chapter up to this point is referred to Barnett (1971), Dumont (1966), Frank (1967), Green (1970), Jalée (1968), Goulet and Hudson (1970) and Worsley (1969).

countries. This, through the efforts of missionaries, colonial governments and international agencies, has long superseded the indigenous systems. These were sometimes, as in India, scholarly and comprehensive, sometimes, as in Africa, well-tuned to the needs of the society. The imported education, however, was attuned to the competitive and materialistic ideologies of the rich nations. This was not changed when it came, so to speak, under local management, for the teachers – however revolutionary in a political sense, had been reared under the same system. Thus when educational enrolments increased astronomically hope did indeed burgeon, but it was hope for gratification based on consumption and concomitantly for jobs, particularly government employment, in the modern sector of the economy. (This latter need had developed in the colonial era, during which the only way to power lay in sharing something of the white man's potency; the habit of associating prestige with these jobs still persists.) This led hundreds of thousands to swarm to the already crowded cities there to live, for the most part, on the fringe of society, a burden to their families, failing to contribute to their struggling nations because jobs have not increased *pari passu* with school enrolments. They have been alienated by their education from their culture; they scorn their unlettered brethren in the village and reject what is still the most important source of wealth and stability in the majority of poor countries – the land.

But a few who are more fortunate or abler make it through elementary and secondary school and end up with university degrees. In the 1950s and early 1960s, when some newly-independent countries (mostly the former French African colonies) literally did not have enough graduates to fill the Cabinet, a B.A. was a guarantee of rapid advancement. Our students in Ghana around this period might easily, within a couple of years of graduation, become ambassadors, ministers, or heads of new government agencies. This was knowledge used to buy into the system with a vengeance. A Harvard degree in law or business administration was as nothing in terms of rapid movement to the top level of the national system, compared with a first degree at

Legon or Ibadan. Nor could it be compared in terms of estrangement from one's background, of acceptance of another civilization. An increasing number of the educated *élites* joined the exploitative network and so throve mightily. Thus by a strange irony, these educational systems which were supported by the colonial regimes because they were a useful sourse of minor functionaries, now provide the necessary servants of neo-colonialism and so are popular targets for international assistance.

I dwell in these pages on questions of development. This might seem remote from our primary concern for education, but in order to consider what education might contribute to development, we have to consider what development might be. This, having attempted to show what it is not, I shall now try to do. In other books (especially Curle, 1971) I have put forward the view that development meant the creation of a form of society in which certain conditions prevailed for human beings. I categorized these as follows:

Safety, in the sense that the society was in general non-violent and that individuals were protected from victimization by the state, or the police, by landlords or by each other – in short that peace prevailed. A corollary of this was undoubtedly that they should have some part in the process of government.

Sufficiency, in the sense that they had enough food, clothing, etc., so that the development of their potentiality was not held back by easily preventable material causes. The level of sufficiency would necessarily vary from place to place. In some cases it might be low by our standards, but the intention is both to safeguard potentiality and to avoid the fallacy that it is only to be achieved (which in any case is only possible for very few) by constantly increasing consumption.

Satisfaction, meaning that life was in general pleasant and that sufficiency was not achieved at excessive psychic and cultural cost.

Stimulus, meaning that the sense of potentiality, intellectual

118

or emotional, social, or spiritual was kept before people's eyes. This perhaps is one of the principal roles of education.

I stress that it will obviously be impossible to achieve these qualities in society without often involving the economy. But economic growth is a means, admittedly an important one, to development: not the end.

Richard Barnett (1971, pp. 27–8) defines development in a manner which is consistent with mine and which delights me, as will be obvious to the reader of this book. 'Development, it cannot be said too often, is the *awakening of awareness*, (my emphasis) literally, an unfolding. A society will develop only as the individuals in it develop their true potential and are prepared to give themselves to social efforts to which they feel personally related and in which they have some rights to control their personal destinies. There is no evidence whatever that the Cadillac showroom a few yards from a rotting slum in the middle of Bangkok or a piece of high technology farm equipment or even an academy award winning Hollywood film stimulates this sort of consciousness.'

Dennis Goulet (1971, pp. 87–95), whose rich and subtle thought does not really bear summary – the reader is recommended to read his book, *The Cruel Choice* – recognizes three universal goals for human life. These are *life-sustenence*, which corresponds somewhat to my concept of sufficiency; *esteem*, the sense of having value, of being respected, of autonomy; and *freedom* from 'servitudes (to nature, to ignorance, to other men, to institutions, to beliefs) considered oppressive.' The realization of these goals constitutes the process of development.

In terms of this approach to development the great difference between the rich ('developed') and the poor ('developing' or 'underdeveloped') nations is that the former at least have the material capacity to achieve developmental goals, especially sufficiency, while the others often do not. What the rich nations lack is the political or moral strength to apply their capacity for the good of all their people.

These views have considerable significance for educational

policy in the poor nations. If development means a quality of human living which is part material (or economic), part cultural and part social (or political), and if education is to contribute thereto, several things follow. Firstly, it must help to nourish the culture. This may mean that it must oppose the alien culture encapsulated in educational practice, or at least present a different model. Secondly, it must contribute in some way towards sufficiency. Here again the implications are forked. Sufficiency depends upon both the skills of people and their attitudes of mind. If their education has decultured them, establishing their aspiration to join the exploitative network, they will not play the social and political parts, nor acquire and exercise the abilities which will raise the sufficiency level of the community (though for one in a thousand it may bring personal affluence). Education, therefore, must provide the appropriate culture and, with the culture, the orientation towards skills and work which will make it possible to reach the necessary material standards. These have already been reached by the rich countries. For this reason, in discussing their educational goals, I concentrate largely on the development of awareness, the eradication of competitive materialism, and so on. These goals are not less important in the poor countries, but to them must be added greater emphasis on building the capacity to achieve sufficiency.

It is hard, however, to break away from the past and envisage a new form of education having elements both indigenous and universal, in which economic and cultural goals are interwoven, which promotes material sufficiency at the same time as it erodes competitive materialism. The past, in fact, is very much embedded in the present, as a glance at the last two or three decades will show us. As recently as the immediate post-World War II period, when university colleges were being set up in what was then British Africa, few African educators thought of anything but emulation of the British model. This, to them *was* education. After years of exceedingly British education, with much wearing of gowns, emphasis on the primacy of Mediterranean civilization, and an all-British curriculum, a strong movement developed for the teaching of African subjects – history, political development, customary law, and the like. But the setting remained British, or French, or whatever it was. The whole ambiance, the administrative and academic hierarchy, the social structure, the values of academic achievement, were and are European. And this is reflected right down through the educational system. When the cry came to Africanize education (or to make it appropriate to the cultural and economic needs of the bulk of the people of Asia, Latin America, or any poor nations of the world instead of an unsuitable copy of something else) few people really knew what this might mean. An obvious implication was to replace white by black teachers, but most of the latter, though nationalistic, had little concept of an education different from that by which they themselves had been moulded. To Africanize or Asianize the curriculum was a step in the right way, but it didn't go nearly far enough. A compulsory course for freshmen in African history and political development did not restore to them the culture of which they had been progressively shorn for the past dozen years by the process of schooling.

Apart from the inertia of tradition, two factors militate against successful localization of education, especially at university level. The first of these is that many subjects are not local but universal, mathematics for example, or the natural sciences. To Africanize science would be to destroy it. It is true that the good teacher will use local materials and examples in his teaching, especially perhaps in biology, but the principles he draws from them are universal. In applied fields such as medicine, localization can and should be carried out without violation of general principles. Nevertheless African medical schools of my acquaintance have in the past concentrated on curative medicine, and the more sophisticated the better. The crying need, however, was for preventative medicine (for decades there would be too few physicians and hospital beds for the treatment of more than a fraction of the sick); for health education, immunization campaigns, better diet, clean water, efficient waste disposal, family planning and population education, anti-malarial measures, etc. The problem in general was, and is, to combine scholarly integrity with attention to the needs and characteristics of the area.

The second difficulty is language. In the Arab and Latin American countries in which there is a single language with a great literature, there is no problem. But what of Nigeria, in which one half of the people speak one of the three main languages and the other half one of about 250 lesser tongues? If you select one language as the medium instruction, even if you teach in the vernacular up to secondary level, may you not alienate those who speak the others? If you use the chief local tongue in each area are you then perhaps fostering a local chauvinism such as led to the recent bloody civil war? How, in any case, could you provide textbooks in all these languages, some of which have never been written? The obvious answer is to use English as a lingua franca which is, moreover, useful in diplomacy and trade. The disadvantage, of course, is that use of the language tends to perpetuate the spirit of the system originated by speakers of the language. In addition, language and culture are closely linked. Words have a symbolic significance relating us to our culture. Unless we have the linguistic genius of a Conrad, a Pole who wrote in English having decided that French was not equally expressive, we lose touch with our culture if we are educated in the tongue of another. But we never become part of that culture either. This is a genuine dilemma, but there are growing efforts to find ways of making it feasible to use the vernacular. In Tanzania, for example, Swahili, the common language of East Africa, has been established not only as the medium of instruction at most levels of education except the university, but also as the national language.

Tanzania is, in fact, almost the only country, which in the spirit of its language policy, has systematically attempted to devise an education to counter the residual effects of colonialism and to promote an appropriate form of development. President Julius Nyerere's philosophy of education and development is lucidly expounded in his own writings. He emphasizes in these that though economic growth is important to the achievement of national goals, it is not to be sought at the expense of human dignity. He stresses also that it is not feasible for a poor country like Tanzania to seek an American or European level of consumption. The country must adjust itself to the fact of its poverty. So far as education is concerned, this means that the schools must not only be largely self-supporting, but must prepare young people, emotionally and technically, for productive rural living. (His philosophy of development is set out in Nyerere, 1968.)

This is the policy which Nyerere called Education for Self Reliance (in Nyerere, 1968; also Resnick, 1968).

The primary schools are to be in and of the community, supported and upheld by it, but also maintaining themselves through selling and consuming what they produce in learning to cultivate the soil and to tend animals. The education given at this level is terminal for the majority, a rounded thing in itself, which prepares young people to lead a constructive rural existence. In this it is unlike many other primary educations which only aim to prepare children for secondary schools which in turn only prepare them for universities, a valid principle if everyone needs and can obtain a higher education, but a wasteful mockery when they do not and cannot.

Promotion to secondary school is not to be simply by examination. Technical ability and social responsibility should also be taken into account. Knowledge, in fact, is treated much less as a commodity than in most systems. Admission into university depends on an estimate, admittedly hard to make, of the number of graduates who can effectively be absorbed into the economy.

There are strong traditions of both co-operation and self-reliance in many African village communities. The weaving of these qualities into the structure of education does more to Africanize it than the teaching of African subjects. It introduces into the educational system the fundamentals of culture: significantly these are also related to the basis of economic life.

In some respects education in Tanzania is still traditional. Refinements of affective education are unknown in most village schools and the relationships of teachers with students are strict and authoritarian. The teaching is formalistic and didactic. The same might be said of other poor countries of which I have had experience – Pakistan, Tunisia, Ghana, Barbados and Venezuela among others to give a wide range of diversity. C. E. Beeby (1966) shows lucidly how this must inevitably be the case, and why pedagogic evolution must be slow. This does not mean to say, however, that such refinements would be undesirable if they could be applied.

But not everything has gone smoothly in Tanzania. Competitive materialism has strong roots and they dig deeper every time a poor African sees a rich one with a smart car or refrigerator, or a rich African sees an even richer European. It could hardly be otherwise. Nevertheless, I believe that Tanzania and other developing countries which adopted her educational developmental policy could take further measures to weaken the hold of consumption values and at the same time to strengthen the economy.

After primary education knowledge once more becomes a commodity. It buys a slice of the system, a slice of power, having implications for consumption capacity. I cannot help fearing that this may eventually reduce the power of Nyerere's noble conception and therefore suggest as an alternative something that could not be done in the over-intricate rich countries for generations, but which might be possible in the simpler economic-educational context of Africa. It would undoubtedly be difficult, even impossible to achieve for political reasons, but possibly some modification of it could be promoted by a skilful leader.

The fundamental proposal would be that payment for work was not determined by the qualifications of the employee or the type of job, but by criteria such as age and family obligations. Thus a cabinet minister might earn less than a truck driver, a clerk more than a physician. This, of course, would not apply to the great majority who are farmers, often at subsistence level, nor to the small minority who are wealthy businessmen. The latter would be (indeed are) heavily taxed on their profits; the former would be assured an adequate living standard in case of difficulty and would be permitted profits on the sale of cash crops which would put them on the same level as salary earners. With economic motivation thus largely removed from work, the incentive would be to do what was interesting, personally rewarding, or socially useful. The educational institutions, as I suggested in Chapter III, would be divided into schools, which were intended to promote personal awareness and growth, and to training institutions, where skills ranging from typing to surgery could be learned.

It is idle to expect education to have an ennobling effect in a society which demeans man by appealing to his greed; schools will then inevitably imitate society. We in the wealthy nations have gone very far towards creating a society in which all parts of the system play on man's rapacity, strengthen his belonging-identity, enhance his ruthless materialism, and bring constant violence to the world. We have also infected the poorer nations, sucking them into the vortex of our economic operations, and educating them with our outlook on life. It is hard to see that we can change ourselves without enormous and unimaginable upheavals, for the tentacles of greed have crept into the very crannies of our hearts. I have greater hopes for Africa, however, and other areas in which the traditions of other civilizations still hold, where the battle with competitive materialism has not been entirely lost. But education alone cannot bring the victory, nor for that matter economics, legislation or political action. Every aspect of life will have to be oriented, with conscious purpose, to the building of a truly peaceful society.

10

Liberation

At the beginning of this book I said that education enslaved and that men and women became free by their own efforts. I intended to convey by this that there is a unique and splendid quality in mankind. Despite the institutions we build and the appalling pressures these exert upon us, driving us to excesses of violence and rapacity, cruelty and self seeking, despite all this, again and again, defying the logic of social and psychological determinism, we are redeemed. We somehow rise above our despairing greed, our frightened need for justification through belonging, the deadening effects of our education, to be magnanimous and compassionate, to sacrifice everything for the good of our fellows. The quality which asserts itself to save us from being machines, completely unaware of themselves and others, driving to destruction, is our humanity.

Perhaps we hardly know what it is to be fully human. We can only guess what it might mean from what we infer from the life of men who have blazed like meteors in the dark skies of our planet, men like Jesus or Gandhi. Nevertheless, we all have the elements of humanity, albeit overlaid and distorted by the exigencies of the system which has been closing in on us, gaining increasing control since our birth. It is perhaps never entirely eradicated, though we live like automata for years. At any moment, something may happen through the agency of who knows what internal or external event, which will blow into flame the dying embers of our humanity. We will become human beings who are aware, capable of objective love, courageous in the defence of truth, careless of our safety and possessions, autonomous.

This is the real liberation and nothing I have said in these pages claims to be a prescription for this unshackling of the human spirit. But there are lesser levels of liberation. What I have been discussing are ways of establishing, so far as education is concerned, conditions in which the breeze may be brought to play on the cinders of humanity, but not the miracle which causes them to burst into flame. Education for liberation is that which attempts to liberate us from the habits of thought, action, and feeling which make us less than human, which enables us in turn to try to liberate others and which transforms the system into the counter-system. But I have argued that education as it mostly constitutes an enslaving subsystem in the large system constructed out of low awareness, the belonging-identity and competitive materialism: and that this system is institutionalized through such mechanisms as the exploitative network, that world-wide arrangement by which the rich and powerful attempt to satisfy, through dominating the poor and weak, the driving desires of competitive materialism and its related psychological mechanisms. The two, the sub-system and the system, depend upon and reinforce each other. If this is true, is it not absurd to consider changing education? Should we not strive to abolish all educational institutes, except the most informal, to de-school society as Ivan Illich advocates? Or if not, should we not simply stand aside and at least avoid complicity?

I can see some attraction to this view, but follow rather his alternative of 'disestablishing schools' (1971a). For one thing, we have schools all around us and they are here to stay for a very long time. Our fulminations will not make them go away. Much better, I believe, to work within them. In this I am encouraged by the words of the great Alan Paton (1971) in accepting an honorary degree at Harvard, 'I understand well (the dissatisfaction of younger people) with the world that we have made, but I do not believe that one can make it any better by withdrawing from it. I understand your argument that if you take part in it, you are only prolonging its existence. I understand your argument that if you take part in it, it will corrupt you just as it has corrupted us. But it is not a very good or a very brave argument. The only way in which one can make endurable man's inhumanity to man, man's destruction of his own environment, is to exemplify in your own lives man's humanity to man and man's reverence for the place in which he lives. It is a hard thing to do, but when was it ever easy to take upon oneself man's irresponsibility for man and his world?'

In addition, I believe that educational institutions are necessary. There is nothing intrinsically bad in grouping people together to learn, through this assembly, like all other human associations, can go wrong. On the contrary, if the principle of schooling is used wisely, humanely, flexibly and efficiently, mankind will be the gainer. There are certain learning problems – but by no means all – which can be solved today by concentration of talent, skills and materials as well as the consistent involvement of persons with the necessary gifts. But the schools of tomorrow – which will undoubtedly be very different from those of today, must of course be detached from the system which presently they serve. I have tried to suggest the first steps by which educators in the exercise of their profession can take to erode attitudes, in themselves and their students, which support the system, and to lay the foundations of a different approach to school and society. If I were a politician, lawyer, engineer, or doctor, I could have said something comparable about another profession, but I have confined myself to what I know.

In conclusion, education for liberation is education which is itself liberated from an improper servitude to a system which values it less for what it contributes to the mind of man than for its service to his greed for power and possessions. Liberated education, released from this thraldom, would be enabled to serve the human spirit. That is its true purpose.

Appendix

I have assumed that the liberation referred to in the title of this book and defined in the last chapter and indeed throughout, is a real and achievable goal: that autonomy is possible. But B. F. Skinner, whose book *Beyond Freedom and Dignity* (1971) appeared when the first draft was completed and whom I greatly admire as a lucid and original thinker, disagrees. Human behaviour, he claims, consists of a series of conditioned responses to the environment whereby we aim to avoid what is unpleasant, or to achieve what is gratifying. Thus freedom, about which we have built so elaborate a mystique, is simply the avoidance of or escape from 'adverse' conditions in the environment, while dignity is what we claim by persuading ourselves that we are not conditioned creatures but are in some fashion solely responsible for our actions. By the same token, the idea of autonomy is no better than a fairy tale.

The ideas on which this book are founded in fact go a long way towards supporting Skinner's position. There is clearly a machine-like quality about a major part of our existence. Our physiological functions, with their subtle impact upon thought and feeling, proceed independently of volition. Anyone capable of honesty with himself must recognize how little conscious control he has over his moods, or the seemingly arbitrary sequence of thoughts which flicker through his mind. Even when he is engaged in some such intellectual activity as giving a lecture, he often 'loses himself' (the phrase is interesting) and talks without really being aware of what he is saying; it is as though he had turned on the appropriate record and gone to sleep. And at another level he must acknowledge the dominating role of chance in his life, from accident of birth onwards. Despite all this he may claim that somewhere within is his real self, his unchanging I, his fundamental and autonomous identity – his dignity, as Skinner puts it; but where is it, how can it be defined?

Man's mechanistic quality, his lack of autonomy, is shown very clearly if we further probe my concept of low awareness and belonging-identity – (my vocabulary is not Skinner's, but up to a point we both say the same thing). A man whose level of awareness is low is by definition one who has no contact with his real self, etc. In a sense it matters little whether he has such a thing or not. He functions as though he did not have one. One characteristic quality of this functioning is that he automatically struggles to escape from those equally automatic (because a product of low awareness) aspects of his makeup which cause him pain or discomfort through guilt, anxiety, sense of inadequacy, worthlessness, futility, impotence and the like. This struggle is primarily manifested through the formation of belonging-identity. These ideas are, of course, parallel to many in psychotherapeutic concepts. It could be said that the man of low awareness is in bondage to certain aspects of his unconscious while the analyst manifests his belief in the healing quality of the ancient maxim, 'know thyself', by helping him to become aware of them. But to the extent that awareness is low, we react to what we do not know about – or very dimly sense. We are being, as it were, pushed around by our unconscious.

A further characteristic of the state of low awareness is that we are dominated successively by a number of 'selves'. Skinner defines a self as 'a repertoire of behaviour appropriate to a given set of contingencies' (p. 199), and goes on to say that we have many such repertoires suitable to various settings. We go through life acting a number of parts evoked by different environments and the actor in each is relatively unknown to the actor in others. We may test this for ourselves. Suppose we awake feeling depressed, but later on (for reasons outside our control) become sanguine and cheerful. In the two moods we are two different people with different sets of views about ourselves, our friends, and the world, different hopes and fears. When we change from one mood to the next, we leave one self behind and cannot really remember it except as in a remote and impersonal fashion, like something read in a book. We say, in wonder, envy or reprobation, 'I don't know what came over me' or, 'I don't know what I was thinking about', meaning that we are no more able to *feel* what it was like to be the former self than to be a completely different individual.

A shift from gloom to elation is, of course, an obvious and fairly extreme case. But we experience innumerable minor moods, each having its own organization and philosophy, which change so softly that we scarcely notice the alteration.

Some psychoanalysts would interpret these selves as related to internalized objects originating in the child's attempts to come to terms with the persons in his environment. They would see a close relationship between the structure of these selves and the anxieties, etc., which impel us to construct the belonging identity in which the selves collaborate. Indeed the connection may be even more complicated and circular, as the following hypothesis suggests; material may be repressed (and thus become the source of anxiety, guilt and the like) because we cannot fully apprehend it if it menaces belonging-identity in a particularly poignant fashion, while belonging-identity is erected as a protection against repressed material. Essentially belonging-identity constitutes an attempt to protect ourselves against feelings which would make us think ill of ourselves, to organize a self-image which will satisfy us that we are indeed worth-while or good human beings possessing, no doubt, dignity and autonomy. It is our response to the lack of (or inability to recognize or be in touch with) an inner self, real I, etc., which should presumably be superior to and capable of controlling the guilt and anxiety-laden lesser facets of our being. Indeed the different selves we portray are largely compounded of different parts of our belonging-identity selected from the available total as the best way of avoiding unpleasantness and achieving gratification in a particular setting.

To refer to autonomy and hence to liberation in these circumstances is meaningless. We are driven by a shifting sequence of fears and pains originating in unknown regions of our being to act through a variety of selves. It would only be possible to talk of autonomy if the self were whole in the sense that unconscious material were available, i.e. were no longer unconscious and that the separate selves or repertoires, if not precisely united, were at least in touch with each other. Only thus could choices be made in which all the evidence were evaluated by all the capacities of the individual. Whether or not one would be justified in referring to such a condition as autonomy or free will is a philosophical question to which I do not have the answer. The constraints would, however, be completely different from those which I just described, or of which Skinner is speaking.

The issue, then, is whether a higher level of awareness is possible – or whether it, too, is another illusion; and whether it could be said to confer a measure of liberation.

Awareness, as I have tried to define it, is a type of linking function both between the levels of consciousness and the component selves. It is a communication system that exists to some extent in us all. Through the functioning of awareness a greater degree of unity (though no doubt never complete) may be achieved. Are there in fact higher and lower levels of awareness? It seems to me self-evident that there are. In the compulsive person who cannot avoid damaging or despiteful behaviour or in the man struggling to give up an undesirable habit there is clearly less contact between the various facets of the personality than is the case in others – the reader may choose his ideal – who are appropriately referred to in contemporary idiom as *together*. If, on the other hand, I say that I am trying unsuccessfully to give up something I really mean that one part of myself is doing so while another part is obviously opposing it. People of higher awareness, when faced with the need for decision, bring to bear upon the problem a far greater proportion of their potential. They are aware of what they are doing when they are doing it.

Skinner observes that the 'accomplished pianist would perform badly if he were as clearly aware of his behaviour as a student who is just learning to play' (p. 193), but this is a misconceived complaint. Part of being aware is to know how we function best, and to play the piano means to utilize the memory of eye and hand without conscious intervention but still to be highly aware of what we are doing and of the quality of the music we are playing. Persons of lower awareness tackle their problems in the limited terms of the currently dominant self evoked for particular protective reasons. The choices made in these circumstances are often disapproved of by subsequent selves. One cannot say that under these conditions a whole person, still less an autonomous one, has been involved in making the decision.

The choices made by the more aware are relatively more objective than those made by the less aware. Decisions of the less aware are made in terms of their subjective needs for gratification or the alleviation of pain in a particular concatenation of circumstances. The more aware are apt to make decisions based on an appraisal of the objective needs of the situation which, being relatively less anchored to their own difficulties, they are able to see more clearly in the present and to project into the future. Thus they tend to serve others rather than themselves.

Here we run into the theory of psychological hedonism. This supports Skinner in asserting that whatever we do is because everything else would be less pleasant; even the suicide who elects a painful death does so because it is preferable to life and because the nature of his dying is the best way to punish those who made his life unbearable. Indeed it is arguable that we only do what is most gratifying to the self; but everything depends upon the size of the self. A narrow and circumscribed self is what we called selfish. A self which is wider and deeper is what we call, paradoxically, selfless, which means that its gratifications are not directly related to the needs of the human being in which it is housed but indirectly through it to the needs of other human beings.

The difference between Skinner and myself is, I believe, that he does not recognize a qualitative difference in the range and state of the self. His fundamental thesis is that certain forms of behaviour can be made more desirable through rewards and others less desirable through punishment. He has no idea of changing the self.

There is also a more subtle difference. I have been writing, for the sake of simplicity, as thought there were a straightforward dichotomy between persons of low and persons of high awareness. But it is more complicated than that. There is also a constantly fluctuating movement between conditions of higher and lower awareness in the same person. Thus we all have, if I may use the term, more autonomous and less autonomous moments. Our selves become related and so expand, giving us wider vision and broader choice, and then contract through separation, becoming sequential and so narrow and rigid.

A final difference between Skinner and me is that whereas he believes in manipulating the environment, I can only see change coming through the raising of the individual's general level of awareness. But Skinner has the last laugh, for whereas he believes he knows how to change the environment, I have only a few inconclusive and unsystematic ideas about increasing awareness.

Bibliography

ALLPORT, G. W. (1955). *Becoming.* New Haven: Yale University Press.

ARDREY, ROBERT (1966). *The Territorial Imperative: A Personal Inquiry into the Animal Origins of Property and Nations.* New York: Atheneum.

BARNETT, RICHARD J. (1971). *Can the United States Promote Foreign Development?* Washington, D.C.: Institute for Policy Studies, mimeo.

BEEBY, C. E. (1966). *The Quality of Education in Developing Countries.* Cambridge, Mass.: Harvard University Press.

BORTON, TERRY (1970). *Reach, Touch, and Teach.* New York: McGraw Hill.

BOSE, NIRURAL KUMART, ed. *Selections from Gandhi.* Available from World Without War Council.

CENTRAL ADVISORY COUNCIL FOR EDUCATION (England, 1967). *Children and Their Primary Schools.* London: Her Majesty's Stationery Office (2 volumes).

COHN-BENDIT, D., *et al.* (1968). *The French Student Revolt.* New York: Hill and Wang.

CURLE, A. and PHILLIP WHITTEN (16 May 1968). *Report on a Study of Academic Programs in the Harvard School of Education.* Cambridge, Mass.: Harvard Graduate School of Education.

CURLE, ADAM (1971). *Making Peace.* London: Tavistock Publications.

CURLE, ADAM (1972). *Mystics and Militants.* London: Tavistock Publications.

DOLCI, DANILO (1969). *The Man Who Plays Alone.* trans. Cowan, New York: Pantheon Books, Inc.

DUMONT, RENÉ (1966). *False Start in Africa.* London: Sphere Books.

FISCHER, LEWIS (1950). *The Life of Mahatma Gandhi.* New York: Harper and Bros.

FRANK, ANDRE GUNDER (1967). *Capitalism and Underdevelopment in Latin America: Historical Studies of Chile and Brazil.* New York: Monthly Review Press. 1967.

FREIRE, PAULO (1970a). *Cultural Action for Freedom.* Cambridge, Mass.: Harvard Educational Review and the Center for the Study of Development and Social Change.

FREIRE, PAULO (1970). *Pedagogy of the Oppressed.* trans. Myra Bergman Ramos. New York: Herder and Herder.

FROMM, ERICH (1957). *The Art of Loving.* New York: Harper & Row, Publishers.

FROMM, ERICH, D. T. SUZUKI, RICHARD DE MARTINO. (1960). *Zen Buddhism and Psycho-analysis.* London: George Allen and Unwin Ltd.

GANDHI, M. K. (1927). *An Autobiography or the Story of My Experiments with Truth.* Ahmedabad, Navajian Publishing House.

GANDHI, M. K. (1950). *Satyagraha in South Africa.* trans. Valji Gouindji Desai, Revised Second Edition. Ahmedabad, Navajivan Publishing House.

GOULET, DENNIS (1971). *The Cruel Choice.* New York: Atheneum.

GOULET, DENNIS and MICHAEL HUDSON (1970). *The Myth of Aid: The Hidden Agenda of the Development Reports.* New York: I.D.O.C. North America.

GREEN, FELIX (1970). *The Enemy Within.* New York: Vintage Books.

GREER, GERMAINE (1970). *The Female Eunuch.* New York: McGraw Hill.

The Graduate Study of Education. Report of the Harvard Committee. Cambridge, Mass.: Harvard University Press. 1966.

GUEVARA, CHE (1967). *Che Guevara Speaks,* Edited by George Lavan. Beverly Hills, California: Merit Publishers.

HESSE, HERMANN (1969). *The Glass Bead Game*, trans. Richard and Clara Wistan. New York: Holt, Rinehart and Winston, Inc. First published in 1943 as *Das Glasperlenspiel*.

HOLT, JOHN (1964). *How Children Fail*. New York: Pitman Publishing Corporation.

HUDSON, LIAM (22 October 1964). 'Academic Sheep and Research Goals'. *New Society*.

ILLICH, IVAN D. (1970). *Celebration of Awareness*. Garden City, New York: Doubleday and Company, Inc.

ILLICH, IVAN D. (19 June 1971a). 'Can we Disestablish Schools or De-School Society?' *Saturday Review*.

ILLICH, IVAN D. (1971). *Deschooling Society*. New York: Harper & Row, Publishers.

JALLE, PIERRE (1968). *The Pillage of the Third World*. New York: Monthly Review Press.

KING, CORETTA (1969). *My Life with Martin Luther King*. New York: Holt, Rinehart and Winston.

KOHL, H. (1969). *The Open Classroom: A Practical Guide to a New Way of Teaching*. New York: New York Review.

KOZOL, JONATHAN (1967). *Death at an Early Age*. Boston: Houghton Mifflin Company.

KUPER, LEO (1957). *Passive Resistance in South Africa*. New Haven: Yale University Press.

LAKEY, GEORGE (1973). *Strategy for the Living Revolution*. New York, Grossman Publishers Inc.

LAKEY, GEORGE and PARKMAN, PAT (16 November 1969). 'El Salvador 1943–44: They Didn't Call it Non-Violence, But –.' *Peace News*.

LIDDELL HART, B. H. (1969). 'Lessons from Resistance Movements – Guerilla and Non-Violent, in Roberts, Adam, ed. (1969).

LORENZ, KONRAD (1965). *On Aggression*. New York: Harcourt, Brace & World, Inc.

JAMES, WILLIAM (1902). *Varieties of Religious Experience*. New York: Modern Library. (Many editions since first published in 1902.)

LUTHULI, ALBERT (1962). *Let My People Go.* New York: McGraw Hill.

LYON, HAROLD C., JR. (1971). *Learning to Feel-Feeling to Learn.* Columbus, Ohio: Charles E. Merrill Publishing Company.

MCCLELLAND, DAVID (1961). *The Achieving Society.* New York: Van Nostrand-Reinhold Books.

MCNEISH, JAMES (1965). *Fire Under the Ashes: The Life of Danilo Dolci.* Boston: Beacon Press.

MASLOW, ABRAHAM H. (1970). *Religions, Values and Peak Experiences.* New York: Viking Press.

MATTHIESSEN, PETER (1969). *Sal si Puedes: Cesar Chavez and the New American Revolution.* New York: Random House.

MEAD, MARGARET (1961). *Cooperation and Competition among Primitive Peoples.* Boston: Beacon Press.

MORRIS, BEN (1972). *Objectives and Perspectives in Education.* London: Routledge and Kegan Paul.

NASH, PAUL (1971). *The Major Purposes of Humanistic and Behavioral Studies in Teacher Education.* Prepared for the working conference of the National Standing Committee on Humanistic and Behavioural Studies in Education, A.A.C.T.E., Washington, D.C. 14–15 April 1971. mimeo.

NYERERE, JULIUS K. (1968). *Ujamaa: Essays on Socialism.* Dar es Salaam: Oxford University Press.

OPPENHEIMER, MARTIN and GEORGE LAKEY (1965). *A Manual for Direction Action: Strategy and Tactics for Civil Rights and All Other Non-Violent Protest Movements.* Chicago: Quadrangle Books.

OTTO, RUDOLPH (1950). *The Idea of the Holy,* Second Edition, trans. by Harvey. London: Oxford University Press.

OUSPENSKY, P. D. (1949). *In Search of the Miraculous.* New York: Harcourt Brace & World, Inc.

PATON, ALAN (June 1971). *Address* at Harvard Commencement Exercises, 17 June 1971; extract quoted in *Harvard Today,* June 1971.

PERLS, F. S., R. F. HEFFERLINE and PAUL GOODMAN (1951).

Gesalt Therapy: Excitement and Growth in the Human Personality. New York: Dell.

RAMSAY, DEBORAH (1971). *Affective Education and Schools.* Cambridge, Mass.: Harvard Graduate School of Education. mimeo.

REICH, CHARLES A. (1970). *The Greening of America.* New York: Random House.

REMINGTON, RUBIN ALISON (1970). *Winter in Prague.* Cambridge, Mass.: M.I.T. Press.

RESNICK, IDRIAN N. (ed.) (1968). *Tanzania: Revolution by Education.* Arusha, Longmans of Tanzania.

ROBERTS, ADAM (ed.) (1969). *Civilian Resistance as National Defence.* Harmondsworth, Penguin Books.

ROBERTS, CARL R. (1969). *Freedom to Learn.* Columbus, Ohio: Charles E. Merrill Publishing Company.

ROGERS, CARL R. (1961). *On Becoming a Person.* Boston: Houghton Mifflin Company.

SCHOLMER, JOSEPH (1955). *Vorduta.* New York: Holt, Rinehart and Winston.

SHARP, GENE (1970). *Exploring Non-Violent Alternatives.* Boston: Porter Sargeant Publishers.

SHARP, GENE (1973). *The Politics of Non-Violent Action.* Boston: Sargent, Porter, Inc.

SILBERMAN, CHARLES E. (1970). *Crisis in the Classroom: The Remaking of American Education.* New York: Random House.

SKINNER, B. F. (1971). *Beyond Freedom and Dignity.* New York: Alfred A. Knopf.

STEIN, ANNIE (May 1971). 'Strategies of Failure'. *Harvard Educational Review,* Vol. 41, No. 2.

WORSLEY, PETER (1969). *The Third World.* London: Weidenfeld and Nicolson.

Subject Index

140

Name Index

144